Jossey-Bass Teacher

Jossey-Bass Teacher provides educators with practical knowledge and tools to create a positive and lifelong impact on student learning. We offer classroom-tested and research-based teaching resources for a variety of grade levels and subject areas. Whether you are an aspiring, new, or veteran teacher, we want to help you make every teaching day your best.

From ready-to-use classroom activities to the latest teaching framework, our value-packed books provide insightful, practical, and comprehensive materials on the topics that matter most to K–12 teachers. We hope to become your trusted source for the best ideas from the most experienced and respected experts in the field.

Strategies for Teaching Adolescents with ADHD

Effective Classroom Techniques Across the Content Areas

Silvia L. DeRuvo

JOSSEY-BASS
A Wiley Imprint
www.josseybass.com

Published by Jossey-Bass
A Wiley Imprint
989 Market Street, San Francisco, CA 94103-1741—www.josseybass.com

Library of Congress Cataloging-in-Publication Data

DeRuvo, Silvia L.
    Strategies for teaching adolescents with ADHD : effective classroom techniques across the content areas, grades 6-12 / Silvia DeRuvo.
        p.   cm.
    Includes bibliographical references and index.
    ISBN 978-0-470-24671-9
    1. Attention-deficit-disordered youth—Education.   2. Educational innovations.   3. Interdisciplinary approach in education.   4. Content area reading.   I. Title.
    LC4713.2.D47   2009
    371.94—dc22

                                                                        2009025577

Printed in the United States of America
FIRST EDITION
PB Printing   10 9 8 7 6 5 4 3 2 1

Contents

3   Research-Based Teaching Strategies: Meeting the Needs of All Learners

7 Creating a Positive Learning Environment for Students with ADHD   105

8 Working Together to Promote Postsecondary Success   121

About This Book

Strategies for Teaching Adolescents with ADHD takes on the challenge you face as teachers in trying to provide meaningful, engaging content-based instruction to meet the needs of your students with ADHD. This book provides insight into the disability of ADHD and how this disability manifests differently in adolescents than in students of other ages. This book also offers extensive insight into the biological and neurological components of ADHD and how weaknesses in executive functions affect not only academic but social and behavioral outcomes for these students as well. Having a clear understanding of ADHD will allow you to better cope with students' needs and proactively plan instruction that meets those needs.

In addition to an understanding of the neurobiological components of ADHD, you need specific research-based instructional strategies that are not formulaic but strategic, focusing on instruction that supports student engagement. The content strategies in *Strategies for Teaching Adolescents with ADHD* provide you, the secondary school teacher, with content-specific ideas in English language arts, math, science, and social studies that allow students to interact with the content through talking, writing, moving, drawing, and creating in a variety of media, all in relation to the content. Further, this book provides you with the effective classroom management structures needed to support an engaging classroom. This book also provides practical strategies for teaching the self-determination skills necessary for those with ADHD and others with mild disabilities to learn the content required for postsecondary education and employment.

About The Author

Silvia L. DeRuvo is a special education resources development specialist with WestEd, a nonprofit agency that works with schools, districts, state agencies, and national policymakers in educational research, products, and programs. Her job focuses primarily on working with schools and teachers on effective research-based instructional practices that support the needs of students with disabilities within integrated classrooms. Prior to her work at WestEd, Silvia was a special educator in elementary schools for two decades and a teacher trainer at California State University, Sacramento. She is a national speaker for the Bureau of Education and Research on topics pertaining to Response to Intervention implementation practices and is a coauthor of *Teaching Young Children with ADHD: Successful Strategies and Practical Interventions for PreK–3,* and *The School Counselor's Guide to ADHD: What to Know and What to Do to Help Your Students,* both published by Corwin Press.

Silvia received an M.A. in communicative disorders from California State University, Fresno, and holds credentials in Multiple Subjects; as a Special Education Specialist: Communications Handicapped; as well as Resource Specialist certification. Silvia lives in Northern California with her husband, two children, a dog, and five cats.

To the Creator who is completing His Work in me

To my family: my husband, Fred, my helpmate and best friend; and Rachel and David, my mature and supportive children. You are all a blessing to me

To the teachers who are not afraid to try these strategies so that their students with ADHD can recognize themselves as capable, effectual learners

Acknowledgments

My deepest thanks and appreciation go to the following people:

Rich Lougy, for first inviting me to coauthor *Teaching Young Children with ADHD: Successful Strategies and Practical Interventions for PreK–3*, and *The School Counselor's Guide to ADHD: What to Know and What to Do to Help Your Students*: I have learned so much from you about individuals with ADHD, and without your expertise and support, I could never have put this book together.

In memory, Bill Harris, who agreed to hire me at California State University, Sacramento, allowing me incredible opportunities to learn from my students.

The students in the special education cohort, Sacramento City Unified School District: You had faith in me, and despite significant challenges, you persevered, listened to me, and implemented many of these strategies in your classrooms. I learned so very much from my time in your classrooms. Thank you.

My students in the general education credential cohort of Project Impact: You also believed what I had to say about effective strategies and inclusion, and you weren't afraid to try. Thank you for your courage. Your students benefited more than you can imagine.

My students and student teachers at California State University, Sacramento: You were not afraid to think outside the box and were willing to implement inclusionary models of special education services because it was best for kids. I learned a great deal from your experiences.

My colleagues at WestEd: You have supported me and provided me opportunities to work with the best of the best from all over the country.

Marjorie McAneny, my editor at Jossey-Bass: I have appreciated your patience, and I know you have done a tremendous amount of behind-the-scenes work to make this book a reality.

My students in Sanger, Clovis, and San Juan Unified: You have been the inspiration for the words written on these pages.

Silvia L. DeRuvo

Chapter 1

Why Another Book on ADHD?

As a secondary teacher, you are a powerful catalyst in the lives of the students who enter your doors. Your extraordinary impact on their success has far-reaching consequences. This book was written to equip you for this weighty responsibility by providing you with a clear understanding of your students with ADHD and how to teach them.

"Succeeding in school is one of the most therapeutic things that can happen to a teenager. In fact, school successes may often be more helpful for students struggling with ADHD than an hour of counseling a week. . . . Teachers are often the critical factor determining the success or failure for students with this condition!"[1] This statement by ADHD expert Chris Zeigler Dendy makes it very clear that it is up to the teacher to make academic success a reality for adolescents with attention-deficit/hyperactivity disorder (ADHD). Secondary students who do not achieve academic success have limited postsecondary options. Teachers face a significant challenge in helping their students with ADHD find academic success at the secondary level. This book was written to give teachers the tools to meet this challenge.

Education in the Twenty-First Century: The No Child Left Behind Act and Federal Accountability

Our nation is in an unprecedented period of focus on education and educational accountability. The sweeping reform created by the No Child Left Behind Act (NCLB) has brought to light the inequalities of education that have persisted for years in this country.

> The sweeping reform created by the No Child Left Behind Act has brought to light the inequalities of education that have persisted for years in this country.

It has been an ongoing unspoken practice to provide a below-average educational experience for students who live in poverty, for students who speak a second language, and for students with disabilities. Students with ADHD were often included in this group of students, those whom Rod Paige, former Secretary of Education, identified as the "most difficult to teach" and were regularly left behind.[2] These students typically did not pass classes, came up credit-deficient due to remedial class attendance, or were unable to pass high-stakes tests—and therefore did not graduate with a diploma. Those who were identified for special education as learning disabled or having other disabilities were often provided a subpar education that did not teach grade-level standards or grade-level skills. Low expectations reigned, and the outcomes were abysmal; 70 percent of adults with learning disabilities were unemployed or underemployed,[3] and the average income for working adults with learning disabilities in 1997 was $20,000 a year.[4]

NCLB has placed a laser-like focus on these inequities and has opened a Pandora's box of previously hidden inequities in the current systems through accountability. Under NCLB, for the first time, all states are being held accountable for the quality of the education they provide to *all* students. Each state has had to develop or adopt a standardized assessment to measure the proficiency of all students on the state's grade-level content standards. NCLB holds the lofty goal that *all* students in each state, in each district, and in each school reach proficiency. This goal includes all students in every classroom, even those "difficult-to-teach" students in your classroom who may have ADHD or other disabilities. Discussion of NCLB often results in the rolling of eyes and the gnashing of teeth, but as former Secretary of Education Margaret Spellings stated in 2006, "What gets measured gets done."[5] This truth cannot be denied. Without the accountability of NCLB, there would continue to be different expectations for different student groups. Realistically, attaining the goal of 100 percent proficiency by 2014 is impossible, but the climb to meet the goal in all states has brought about profound changes in the way that teachers teach and in instructional opportunities for all students.

The Individuals with Disabilities Education Act of 2004

It is possible that the most pronounced change caused by NCLB has been for students with disabilities. The spotlight on the performance of these students has revealed that the educational outcomes for students with disabilities have not been held to the same standard as those for their peers. "Special education classification has too frequently been used to diminish the expectations for the students designated as eligible for such services and to minimize the responsibility of general education teachers and administrators for their progress."[6] The pervasiveness of lowered expectations and below-average educational opportunities has been brought to light.

The fact that, in the past, special education has existed in its own separate silos has contributed to the marginalization of special education students. In the typical approach to special education, children are not seen as students first but rather as part of a separate system in which labels have determined both the access to grade-level content and the instruction itself.

In conjunction with NCLB, the Individuals with Disabilities Education Act of 2004 supports the notion that students with disabilities can be proficient at grade-level standards when provided instruction in the general education curriculum. This is a far cry from the traditional special education practices of self-contained classrooms with a separate curriculum or resource rooms with remedial instruction. The combined effect of these two acts has broken down the silo mentality of separate systems and has created educational scenarios in which all teachers are responsible for all students, providing an integrated schoolwide instructional program in which all students have access to standards-aligned instruction in the general education core classroom (see Figure 1.1).

> Educational equity for students with disabilities has not been an option in the past.

Students with ADHD and Special Education: Section 504 of the Rehabilitation Act of 1973

Prior to the reauthorization of the Individuals with Disabilities Education Act (IDEA) in 1997, the only statutory option for obtaining educational support for students with ADHD was Section 504 of the Rehabilitation Act of 1973. IDEA 1997 allowed students with ADHD who were *significantly impaired* to qualify for special education services under the "Other Health Impaired" (OHI) federal handicapping condition category [34 CFR §300.8(c)(9)]. Most students with

Not Integrated

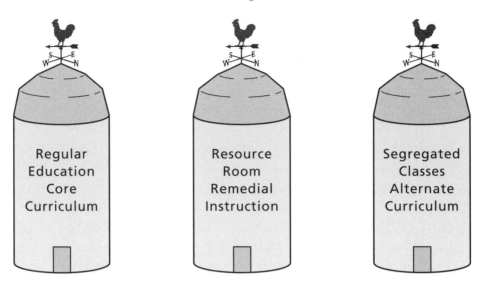

Integrated

Figure 1.1: Nonintegrated and Integrated Approaches to Instruction

Source: Illustration created by Fred DeRuvo.

ADHD do not qualify as having an OHI handicapping condition because the impairment is often not deemed significant enough to warrant special education services; however, instructional accommodations and adaptations provided through a Section 504 plan are considered to be *required* for the student to be academically successful.

While most students with ADHD in a typical classroom function without the intensive, specially designed academic instruction or supplementary services provided by special education under IDEA, many students are affected to the extent that they require a Section 504 plan of some sort. Section 504 of the Rehabilitation Act of 1973 is a civil rights law that prohibits discrimination or harassment on the basis of a disability in any program receiving federal financial assistance. Therefore, public schools must comply with the nondiscrimination requirements of Section 504 to provide students with disabilities with a "free and appropriate public education" in a program designed to meet the students' educational needs as adequately as they meet the educational needs of students without disabilities. This statute (Section 504, 34 CFR § 104) identifies an "individual with a disability," as a person who "has a physical or mental impairment which substantially limits one or more major life activities."

- "Major life activities" is defined as functions such as caring for one's self, performing manual tasks, walking, seeing, hearing, speaking, breathing, *learning*, and working.

- "Substantially limits" describes a disability that significantly affects the *student at school*.

- "Meeting the students' educational needs as adequately as they meet the educational needs of students without disabilities" refers to educating students in a general education classroom with the use of supplementary or related aids and services. These accommodations are identified in the student's Section 504 plan and might include a change in the educational setting or materials or strategies that do not significantly alter the content of the curriculum or the level of expectation of a student's performance but that *allow the student to access the general education curriculum*.

Because learning is one of the major life activities identified in this law, students diagnosed with ADHD whose ability to be in school and do their schoolwork is substantially limited by their disability are found to be eligible for academic accommodations under Section 504.

Not every student with ADHD will have a 504 plan, but those who find that their disability substantially limits their ability to be successful in school will. There continues to be some confusion in the field about whether providing the accommodations to the student are a district's, school's, or individual instructor's choice. Under the law, it is clear that the provisions are not optional. If the student has been assessed by a qualified professional and is found to qualify as a person with a disability under Section 504, then that student's district, school, and individual instructors must provide the accommodations identified by the school's 504 team and included in the 504 plan.

The 504 team, including the site administrator or that person's designee, general education teachers, school psychologist or other specialists, parents, and the student determine which accommodations would allow the student to be free from discrimination and have the same instructional opportunities as his peers without the disability. An example of a reasonable accommodation for a student with ADHD who struggles with the organizational skill of lining math problems up correctly on a blank piece of paper would be to provide the student with a sheet that has the problems already written on it or with graph paper that would help the student with the organization needed to write the problems correctly. For note taking, the student might be provided with a graphic organizer or a note-taking guide. These simple examples show that the accommodations in a 504 plan are often easily implemented and do not require an inordinate amount of work or planning on the part of the school or the instructor, but nonetheless can have a significant impact for a student who might get the math answers wrong due to poor alignment on the page or have poor study notes due to difficulties in keeping up with note taking.

All teachers and staff working with the student should be informed of the 504 accommodations, and the student should be able to advocate for these herself. Once a district, school, or instructor is informed of the accommodations in the plan, it is a breach of the student's civil rights to disallow the use of them. Compliance with the law requires that teachers, students, and staff recognize that accommodations are not optional because the disability puts the student at a disadvantage; the accommodations in the 504 plan simply level the playing field, creating a more equitable educational opportunity for young people with ADHD.

> It is a breach of a student's civil rights to disallow the use of accommodations.

Students identified as having ADHD whose disability significantly affects their academic progress to the extent of requiring specially designed academic instruction or supplementary services under IDEA will also have accommodations written into their Individualized Education Plan (IEP). In the same vein as 504 plans, these accommodations are deemed by the IEP team as necessary in order for the student to make progress in the general education curriculum. It would be a breach of IDEA to deny these accommodations that are provided to the student by law.

Teaching in the Twenty-First Century: Current Research and Instructional Practice

To a secondary school teacher, meeting the mandates of NCLB, IDEA 2004, and Section 504 of the Rehabilitation Act may seem overwhelming. Making sure that no student in your class is left behind and that all students, including your students with ADHD, meet grade-level standards is quite a challenge. This book has been written to support you, the secondary school teacher, in reaching these lofty, yet attainable goals.

First, as a teacher of young adults with ADHD, it is important that you be able to recognize how the disability may look in your classroom. Although you may have friends or relatives who have a child with ADHD, the symptoms of this disability may look very different in your secondary school classroom. It is also essential that you realize that the single label *ADHD* actually includes behaviors that differ from student to student and from gender to gender. Having a clear understanding of the neurobiological and neurological components of the disability may give you more clarity on the puzzling behaviors of some of your students. The next chapter will focus on what ADHD means for adolescents with this disability and what it may look like in your classroom.

Abundant research supports the proposition that engaged students learn more, and there is a direct correlation between the amount of time that students are actively engaged in learning and their achievement levels.[7] Instruction that is engaging will produce better outcomes for students with ADHD as well as reduce many of their common behavior problems. Chapter Three will focus on instructional engagement strategies that allow students to be continually involved in their learning, thus improving their academic level and their psychological investment in meeting grade-level standards.

Differentiated Instruction

Differentiated instruction is focused to meet the specific learning needs and learning styles of all students. Our highly technological society has changed the way that students learn and take in information. Students are technologically connected in ways that most parents and teachers cannot comprehend. Is it any wonder that the traditional form of classroom instruction has become obsolete? The time has come to break the paradigms of our old instructional models and methods and embrace student-centered, active learning and engaging instructional methods. Chapter Three will also examine specific research-based instructional strategies that will support the instructional needs of your YouTube-generation students and the students with ADHD in your classroom.

The Student-Centered Classroom

Teaching in the twenty-first century requires a culture in which the focus has changed from what is taught to what is learned. Chapter Four defines the student-centered classroom, which is a major shift from the teaching of content to the teaching of students. In a student-centered classroom, the teacher facilitates the learning, but the students do the critical thinking work, solving problems through discussion and joint efforts. Students with ADHD flourish in a student-centered environment because the activities of the class have meaning and allow them to take greater ownership of their learning.

Within the context of a learning-centered classroom, research-based instructional strategies for English language arts will be examined in Chapter Four. This chapter investigates specific vocabulary instruction strategies, reading comprehension strategies, and classroom practices that motivate students with ADHD to become actively involved in literacy. Reading intervention structures and processes are also discussed, as well as specific scaffolds for developing independent writing skills in students who struggle with working memory.

High-level math skills are a gateway skill to higher education. Because a large number of students with ADHD have difficulty in learning math due to issues with working memory that affect their ability to memorize and recall information, it is essential for the twenty-first-century teacher to use instructional strategies that address these weaknesses. In Chapter Five, we will look at the different levels of math knowledge required to be successful in math and how ADHD affects these processes. The chapter also takes an in-depth look at seven instructional strategies for students who are at risk for math failure that were identified by the Center on Instruction. Strategies for accessing algebraic concepts will also be covered, including the use of the concrete-representational-abstract (CRA) instructional strategy to help students learn how to translate word problems into mathematical symbols and link the concrete to a representation and then to an abstract or symbolic level. Effective strategies to help with memory and recall, such as graphic organizers, mnemonics, and process steps, will also be discussed.

Standards-Aligned Instruction

The application of standards-aligned instruction in science and social studies is the focus of Chapter Six. When focusing on standards instead of textbooks and defining the curriculum as a structured set of learning outcomes, teaching these two content areas can be a very creative endeavor. This chapter will look at the latest research on effective science and social studies instruction within the context of a learner-centered classroom in which active learning and intentional student engagement are employed. This chapter will look at the motivational factors that affect students with ADHD when learning the content in these two areas as well as ideal processes for eliciting intellectual engagement. Examples from teachers who have made science instruction intellectually engaging and who have brought history alive are provided in this chapter as well as a few teacher tricks for helping students memorize basic science and history facts.

Response to Intervention: Behavioral and Academic Approaches

Students with ADHD often suffer from anxiety disorders[8] and find the unpredictability of teachers' behavioral expectations across a school campus too confusing to figure out, often leaving students lost, confused, or unresponsive. Students with ADHD need consistency and predictability as well as rituals and routines that support positive behavioral interactions with their teacher and other students. Developing schoolwide supports for positive behavior that include clear common expectations is covered in Chapter Seven. This chapter will cover the behavior management strategies that do not work as well as those that have proven to be successful. Chapter Seven also looks at proactive strategies for managing students' behavior and at the principles of fairness and respect. Finally, this chapter covers the three tiers of behavior intervention that are often referred to as a *multi-tiered intervention* or a *Response to Intervention model*. Strategies that support students at all levels of behavioral needs will be investigated, as well as what can be done for students with ADHD who need the highest level of behavioral intervention.

Secondary school teachers have a tremendous responsibility for meeting the academic, social, and behavioral needs of their students with ADHD. Chapter Eight covers the schools' responsibility for providing equitable educational opportunities for all students through a multi-tiered intervention or Response to Intervention (RtI) model. This chapter will explore the different purposes of RtI and how students with ADHD can benefit from each tier of intervention, depending on their particular academic needs. Finally, this chapter looks at the responsibility of the family and, ultimately, of the student. Students with ADHD at the secondary level need to be able to advocate for their own needs, but beyond that, they need to develop long-term strategies that will build self-determination and effective transition skills. This chapter investigates classroom activities that help students with ADHD develop these skills, which will serve them throughout life.

> It is the school's responsibility to provide equitable educational opportunities for all students through a multi-tiered intervention or Response to Intervention (RtI) model.

To Sum Up

Facing the changes created by NCLB and its subsequent accountability for all students is not easy. The shift in responsibility and instructional practice is uncomfortable for many teachers. Recognizing this discomfort is the first step in moving forward and taking the steps necessary to bring about necessary change. The information and strategies provided in this book provide an opportunity to empower teachers to take on the challenge of change. Recognizing the specific needs of students and having the tools, knowledge, and strategies to adjust instruction to meet those needs will create classrooms where productive learning will occur. This book aims to provide you, the secondary school teacher, with the tools, knowledge, and strategies you need to make productive learning a reality for your students.

Chapter 2

Understanding ADHD in Adolescents

Having ADHD puts kids at risk for problems at school, academically, socially, and behaviorally. Middle school and high school are often the most challenging years of these kids' lives. These students often were supported by the structure of the elementary school classroom, but once they find themselves at middle school, the barrage of change and juggling of teachers, classes, homework, and assignments becomes overwhelming and grades often make a very quick downward spiral. A teacher can make a significant impact on changing the trajectory of this spiral. Teachers are very influential in the lives of teenagers, and when teachers believe in them and give them respect and esteem, they respond in kind. "When a teacher conveys a message that a teenager is capable and worthwhile, the teen believes the message."[1]

Teachers want their students with ADHD to succeed but often feel ill equipped to do so. This book has been written to give those teachers not only the tools to teach but also a greater understanding of who their students with ADHD are and what the "hidden disability" of ADHD really means for them.

Willful Disobedience or Neurobiological Disorder?

Many students with ADHD have been accused of "willful disobedience," "defiance," "laziness," or outright "rebellion." Did these students choose to not follow directions or not complete their projects on time, or is their lack of ability to follow through due to a neurobiological disorder? Research has shown that for students with ADHD, there are some changes in the brain that are not present in nonaffected students. Positive emission tomography (PET) scans have shown some differences in the brains of students with ADHD, including reduced metabolic activity in the frontal areas of the brain that are involved in attention, impulsivity, motor activities, emotions, and memory.[2]

The variability of symptoms in individuals with ADHD can be explained in part by anomalies in these different parts of the brain's circuitry. Students with ADHD who show decreased metabolic activity in the areas of the brain that are thought to be responsible for the regulation of inhibition and attention will exhibit ADHD symptoms due to abnormalities in neurotransmitter functioning. The abnormal functioning of these neurotransmitters affects the proper functioning of areas of the brain that regulate attention, impulse control, and so on.[3] The two primary neurotransmitter systems most directly involved in ADHD are dopamine and norepinephrine systems. These two systems influence a variety of ADHD-like behaviors, including those involving attention, inhibition, motor activity, and motivation.

Understanding the Nerve Cell

In order to clearly understand how neurotransmitters affect the behavior of students with ADHD, it is essential to understand the function of the nerve cell (see Figure 2.1). The nerve cell is the holder of neurotransmitters and the roadway on which messages pass through the central nervous system. Communication within the nerve is electrical, but between nerves, it is chemical. The electrical impulse in the nerve signals the chemical release of neurotransmitters from the cell into the synaptic cleft—the space between one nerve cell's terminal end and the other nerve cell. The released neurotransmitters then bind to the receptor on the next cell, creating an electrical impulse. This transmission of the neural impulse across the synaptic cleft from nerve to nerve is how information is passed from one nerve cell to potentially millions of cells in the central nervous system.[4] Deficiencies in these neurotransmitters will exhibit themselves in the signs and symptoms of ADHD.[5]

When abnormalities exist in these systems of neurotransmitters, teachers observe that their adolescents with ADHD struggle with listening, finishing work, irritability, or sleepiness in class. Academically, students with ADHD may struggle with comprehending what they read, memorizing facts, organizing thoughts for writing, or using their working memory to solve math problems.[6]

Although the perception among the general public is that all students with ADHD exhibit hyperactive behavior, this characteristic is found in only about half of those identified with this disorder. In adolescents, this particular characteristic

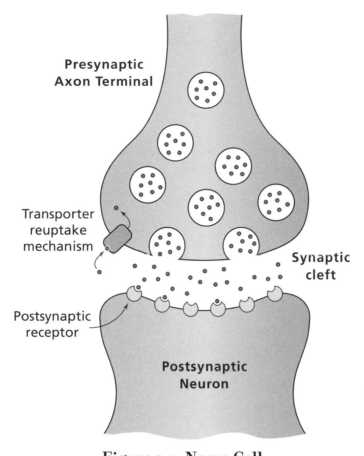

Figure 2.1: Nerve Cell

Source: Used with permission, Hope Press.

is even less prevalent, making a misdiagnosis of willful defiance or disorderly conduct all too common for students who have ADHD but do not exhibit the hyperactive behaviors. Even medical diagnosticians often overlook the fact that students with ADHD might not move around their office any more than any other teen during an office visit for a diagnosis. Often, these students without hyperactivity are not diagnosed in elementary school, but begin to exhibit problems in middle school. This is one reason that thorough evaluation of observational records of the student's long-term behavior is important in determining the presence or the absence of ADHD and its symptoms.

Types of ADHD

As an educator at a secondary school, you may not have had the same amount of experience as your elementary-level colleagues in dealing with "typical" students with ADHD. At the elementary level, students with ADHD are difficult to miss because their overactivity and impulsivity make them extremely recognizable.

Secondary school students with ADHD may look significantly different, and understanding these primary symptoms as well as what the clinical definitions describe will help you to recognize students with ADHD in your classroom so that you can provide them with the support and accommodations they need in order to find success.

Primary Symptoms of ADHD

The primary symptoms of ADHD are *inattention*, *hyperactivity*, and *impulsivity*. These behaviors will be seen in varying degrees in students diagnosed with the disorder, making it difficult to diagnose, given that no two students with ADHD will have the exact same behaviors or academic difficulties. Because the symptoms of ADHD undergo developmental changes as children mature, students with ADHD are often not recognized as having the disorder as they progress through secondary schools, and their inattentive behaviors are most often attributed to laziness or lack of motivation.[7]

Most students with significant ADHD symptoms are diagnosed during their elementary school years. It is during these early years that the hyperactive attribute of ADHD is most prevalent and parents and teachers follow through on the appropriate steps to diagnosis. These students are most often identified as a result of their excessive motoric behaviors and distractibility in the classroom. These overt behaviors are easily recognized, as are the subsequent academic and behavioral issues that further aid in the appropriate diagnosis of ADHD. If students have not been previously diagnosed, often the absence of such hyperactive behaviors in adolescents makes diagnosis difficult to obtain, leaving many students undiagnosed.

Secondary school teachers may have a difficult time recognizing ADHD behaviors in their classroom because not all students present ADHD in the same way or to the same degree, and the manifestation of the associated behaviors may change over time. In order to better grasp what these behaviors may look like, it is important to know what behavior constitutes an ADHD diagnosis.

Defining ADHD

The current diagnosis of ADHD is divided into four categories in the *Diagnostic and Statistical Manual of Mental Disorders* (DSM-IV-TR) of the American Psychiatric Association (2000). Although students may have characteristics of each category, the diagnosis will fall under the heading that best represents their behaviors.[8] The four subtypes are:

- **Attention-deficit/hyperactivity disorder, predominantly inattentive type.** This diagnosis applies to students who are inattentive but do not have problems with restlessness or hyperactive or impulsive behaviors.[9] These students are the daydreamers, the underachievers, unfocused and unable to complete assignments. These students may be internally distracted, but this is not always evident to teachers.

- **Attention-deficit/hyperactivity disorder, predominantly hyperactive-impulsive type.** This diagnosis applies to students who are more hyperactive and impulsive than their developmental level warrants. In teenagers, hyperactive behavior is often replaced with restlessness.[10] These students do not usually struggle with attention.[11] This population of students has the most difficulties with behavior in school and in the community.

- **Attention-deficit/hyperactivity disorder, combined type.** This diagnosis applies to students who have difficulty with both inattention and hyperactivity or restlessness. Most of these students do not have issues with impulsivity.[12]

- **Attention-deficit/hyperactivity disorder, not otherwise specified (NOS).** This population of adolescents and adults do not meet the full criteria for ADHD but still have some of the symptoms of inattention, restlessness, or impulsivity. They are often diagnosed with either ADHD-NOS or with "ADHD in Partial Remission."[13]

In order to meet the requirements for an ADHD diagnosis, students must have six of the nine characteristics in either the "Inattention" section or the combined "Hyperactivity" and "Impulsivity" sections and must exhibit these behaviors in more than one environment.

Symptoms of ADHD as Described in the DSM-IV-TR

Inattention

- Often fails to give close attention to details or makes mistakes in schoolwork or other activities
- Often has difficulty sustaining attention in tasks or play activities
- Often does not seem to listen when spoken to directly
- Often does not follow through on instructions and fails to finish schoolwork, chores, or duties in the workplace (not due to oppositional behavior or failure to understand directions)
- Often has difficulty organizing tasks and activities
- Often avoids, dislikes, or is reluctant to engage in tasks that require sustained mental effort (such as schoolwork and homework)
- Often loses things necessary for tasks or activities at school, at home, or in the workplace (for example, school assignments, pencils, books, or tools)
- Is often easily distracted by extraneous stimuli

- Is often forgetful of daily activities

Hyperactivity (These behaviors may have been exhibited in elementary school)

- Often fidgets with hands or feet or squirms in seat
- Often leaves seat in classroom or other situations in which remaining seated is expected
- Often runs or climbs excessively in situations where it is inappropriate (in adolescents or adults, may be limited to subjective feelings of restlessness)
- Often has difficulty playing or engaging in leisure activities quietly
- Is often "on the go" or often acts as if "driven by a motor"
- Often talks excessively

Impulsivity

- Often blurts out answers before questions have been completed
- Often has difficulty awaiting a turn
- Often interrupts or intrudes on others (for example, butts into conversations or games)

Source: Adapted from American Psychiatric Association, 2000.

The reported prevalence of ADHD ranges from 3 percent to 20 percent; most experts accept a range of 3 percent to 7 percent,[14] meaning that most teachers will have at least one student with ADHD on one of their class rosters. They will find that boys are more frequently diagnosed with ADHD, although research points to the fact that girls are underdiagnosed because they often do not exhibit the hyperactive behavior so often associated with ADHD.

ADHD in Girls

Over the years, girls with ADHD have often been overlooked because the focus in diagnosis has been the classic symptoms of hyperactivity and impulsivity, although some girls do exhibit these behaviors. In the field trials of the *Diagnostic and Statistical Manual of Mental Disorders* (DSM-IV) for all children identified with ADHD, 20 percent of the hyperactive-impulsive group, 27 percent of the inattentive group, and 12 percent of the combined group were girls.[15] Studies to date indicate that girls with inattentive type are probably underdiagnosed due to the absence of the ADHD behaviors that are typically a critical factor in diagnosis. Girls with ADHD often have more problems with the focused and selective components of attention. In the classroom, teenage girls with ADHD appear sluggish and less accurate in information processing, and they exhibit memory retrieval problems; in regard to their social development, they are often seen as shy, withdrawn, reticent, and apprehensive. In addition, they often exhibit anxiety and mood disorders such as depression and anxiety.[16]

Because ADHD is a genetic disorder, it is present from birth. For girls, the symptoms may not become apparent until puberty, when the demands of school and the need for organization and performance increase. Poor executive functions that may have always been present do not become evident until tasks that tax these executive functions are required as part of the middle school experience. This change in demand for organization, and multitasking, as well as the need to develop and stick to long-range plans, makes the ADHD symptoms of inattention more apparent. Teachers and parents often report that around puberty is when they see an increase in irritability and mood swings as well.[17]

> For girls, the symptoms of ADHD may not become apparent until puberty when the demands of school and the need for organization and performance increase.

These changes in behavior and emerging difficulties in school during the middle school years often result in a referral for assessment for learning disabilities. Unfortunately, only the poor academic achievement is assessed, still leaving out the assessment for ADHD. "In many cases, the poor academic achievement is attributed to the thought that some girls are just not as bright or academically capable as others."[18] This perpetuates the perception of some girls as "airheads," negatively affecting their self-esteem and blunting their awareness of their own capabilities. Adolescent girls will often then identify themselves with this airhead persona and will fulfill the underachievement prophesy that the persona entails.

Girls suffer from ADHD differently from boys as well. Girls with ADHD are less likely to be hyperactive but twice as likely to suffer from depression.[19] These girls feel the disappointment of their lack of social acceptance much more than boys do. They struggle with recognizing social cues, often alienating their classmates, which results in their having few friends and leads to loneliness and despair. In addition, they often suffer from anxiety that can turn into checking behavior because of their fear of forgetting things. Their struggle with racing thoughts may leave them unfocused and unable to remember. Their poor executive functions keep them from being able to prioritize the most important thoughts or actions, leaving them paralyzed and helpless and exacerbating their anxiety.

> Girls suffer the consequences of ADHD differently from their male counterparts.

Although not much research has been done on girls with ADHD, research done at the University of Virginia and the Stanford University School of Medicine identified common characteristics of teenage girls with ADHD. Both studies found that older girls often internalized their feelings, resulting in withdrawal, physical complaints, social problems, anxiety, and depression.[20] Adolescent girls with ADHD were also more likely to develop body image dissatisfaction and go through the repeated cycles of binge eating and purging behaviors common in bulimia nervosa. Girls with ADHD are often impulsive in their behavior, causing problems with healthy eating and healthy weight. The resulting negative body image leads to the binging and purging symptoms. Surprisingly, older girls often had relatively high verbal IQ scores, which act as a barrier to ADHD diagnosis.[21]

Understanding ADHD in Adolescents

These girls do not fit the model of academic failure because their impulsivity pushes them to be overachievers and people pleasers. They know that something is not right, but they internalize their struggles and are determined in their checking behaviors, driven by anxiety to keep themselves from academic failure. Because girls who fit this profile do well in school, it is highly unlikely that they will ever receive a proper diagnosis.

Teachers need to be aware that adolescent girls with ADHD may display behaviors outside of the standard ADHD symptoms and should be cognizant that eating disorders, anxiety, and depression in their female students may be due to ADHD.

Kathleen Nadeau provides a clearer picture of ADHD in females.[22] She describes girls with ADHD, using the three ADHD subtypes. She describes the inattentive types as the daydreamers who are often overlooked. These are the girls who often exhibit anxiety and depression. In addition to being overlooked, their intelligence is often underestimated. The hyperactive-impulsive girls are the tomboys who are often involved in sports and work very hard to please their teachers and parents. They are often seen as nonacademic and undisciplined. The combined types, those with both inattention and hyperactivity-impulsivity are referred to as "chatty Kathys." The hyperactivity in these girls is often manifested in overemotionalism, excitability, and a silly personality that hides disorganized thoughts. These girls are often identified as being hyper-talkative and extremely social, often engaging in risky behaviors at an early age. These girls often realize that something is wrong, but without a diagnosis, they try to internalize their feelings of inadequacy, which often leads to guilt and shame, a common denominator in young women with ADHD.[23]

The Impact of ADHD on Adolescents

The impact of ADHD on adolescents is far-reaching. As mentioned earlier, recognizing the student with ADHD in your classroom is the first step in being able to provide them with the supports and accommodations that they desperately need. Recognizing the behaviors and academic indicators of ADHD in adolescents will further inform your ability to more specifically meet their individual needs.

Hyperactive Students

As we have seen in the behaviors of girls with ADHD, the adolescent student with ADHD is probably no longer running uncontrollably around the room but may still be moving through foot tapping, leg bouncing, pencil tapping, desk drumming, humming, or other movements that might be irritating to those sitting around him. Such a student is usually unaware of this constant motion and is not doing it willfully or consciously. Allowing this student to continue to tap or bounce his leg is one way to respect his disability. If desk drumming or pencil tapping is too loud during instruction, request that the student tap the pencil on his own leg or provide him with a Koosh Ball or other item that he can quietly use to keep his hands busy.

In addition to the motoric activity, students with ADHD struggle with keeping focused on the most important information. Their scattered thoughts cause them to go off on tangents that take them away from instruction. Students with ADHD may grapple with rapidly firing thoughts that keep them from attending to one thing for any length of time. Students equate this to a small rubber ball bouncing off the walls of a racquetball court.[24] The thoughts are erratic and can go on bouncing crazily for a long time before the students recognize that their thoughts are off track and need to be brought back. This is not an easy task, and for some students, slowing their thinking down is nearly impossible when they are required to sit quietly.

Inattentive Students

Like girls with ADHD, students with the inattentive type of ADHD are the ones who often go undiagnosed. They are the daydreamers who are often considered lazy or sluggish and are perceived as underachievers. Such an unfocused student is internally distractible and finds it hard to bring her attention back once it has wandered off. She is dealing with internal distractibility that makes it hard for her to block out information that is not important. She is distracted by the hum of the lights, the noises in the hall, and the roar of the lawn mower, as well as the visual information that bombards her from all around. She is distracted by the clothes the teacher is wearing, the glasses on her face, her eyebrows, and her earrings. She may also be distracted by the tag on the back of her shirt and the seam of her socks in her shoes. All this information is vying for her attention internally, and she has to be able to push it to the back of her mind in order to discern and focus on the important information.

Such a student will sometimes be seen in a high school classroom with her head on her desk and her eyes closed. To most teachers, this is unacceptable and repeated attempts are made to get the student to put her head up and look at the teacher. Unfortunately, as soon as the student complies, all the sensory information begins to flood in again and the student again finds herself trying to block out the less important information. Sometimes when her head is on her desk, the student is attempting to shut out the extraneous information so that she can attend to the teacher's voice. It may be a reasonable accommodation to allow her to use this method to attend, especially if she can follow along with discussions that way. This student might also be found doodling on her notebook or in her notes. Again, she may be attempting to block out extraneous information and focus her attention on listening.

Academic Indicators of ADHD

We now know that most adolescents with ADHD will not be running around the room or climbing on the furniture like their younger counterparts, but they have common behaviors that will help you identify students who may have ADHD in your classroom. Chris Zeigler Dendy, in her book *Teaching Teens with ADD and ADHD: A Quick Reference Guide for Teachers and Parents*,[25] identifies some of the following behaviors as indicators of ADHD:

Inattention often looks like:

- Difficulty listening in class and daydreaming
- Lack of attention to detail, careless mistakes, not cognizant of errors
- Difficulty completing tasks and staying focused on work
- Lack of awareness of grades

Impulsivity often looks like:

- Rushing through work without reading directions, taking shortcuts, answering carelessly
- Difficulty with delayed gratification

Poor organizational skills often look like:

- Difficulties with organizing materials, homework, assignments, etc.
- Difficulties with organizing and sequencing thoughts
- Difficulty starting new tasks
- Difficulty breaking tasks into doable parts
- Difficulty sequencing steps in a task
- Difficulty planning ahead for long-term assignments

Impaired sense of time may look like:

- Difficulty with accurately judging time causing tardiness, and difficulty with patience when waiting
- Difficulty with managing time, not having an accurate sense of how long tasks will take
- Procrastinates and puts off assignments until the last minute
- Weak time-management skills
- Difficulty with developing timelines for completion of schoolwork

Why Do Adolescents with ADHD Struggle?

Recent brain research has provided insight into the complexity of ADHD in young people. This research has identified the integral role of executive functions in helping the student meet the myriad of daily demands for thinking, organizing, focusing, persevering, regulating, and retrieving information that must be fulfilled in order to be academically successful. While medication has provided many students with relief from some of their ADHD symptoms, executive function weaknesses are not alleviated through medical intervention. Given that this is the case, it is imperative that as a teacher of students who exhibit these weaknesses, you understand the role that executive function weaknesses play in the academic functioning of your students.

The Role of Executive Functions

Within an adolescent's brain, executive functions operate as the brain's CEO in helping to manage and regulate behavior.[26] Executive functions play an important role in performing many of the tasks necessary for academic success. Thomas Brown, an expert in ADHD, identifies six clusters of executive functions that are often impaired in students with ADHD:

1. *Activation:* organizing, prioritizing, and activating work
2. *Focus:* focusing, sustaining, and shifting attention to task
3. *Effort:* regulating alertness, sustaining effort, and processing speed
4. *Emotion:* managing frustration and modulating emotions
5. *Memory:* utilizing working memory and accessing recall
6. *Action:* monitoring and self-regulating action

Although adolescents with ADHD may not be impaired in all areas, most will have difficulties with at least some aspect of each of these clusters.[27]

> Executive functions operate as the brain's CEO in helping to manage and regulate behavior.

The Effects of Weaknesses in Executive Functions

Once you have an understanding of the effects of executive function weaknesses in your students with ADHD, many of their puzzling behaviors will begin to make sense. Their seemingly willful lack of follow-through and their incredible issues with organization and perseverance will be clearly understood as a part of their disability rather than a character flaw. This type of understanding is a true gift to the student with ADHD who struggles with weaknesses in these areas.

Activation

Weaknesses in activation cause the student to struggle with procrastination, especially if the task is not particularly interesting. Students with weaknesses in activation have extreme difficulty with getting started on tasks even when they know what they need to do, and they often wait until it is an "emergency" before they get started. They struggle with organizing themselves and paying attention to detail, and they have a poor sense of time and how long it takes to complete a task.

Focus

Those who struggle most with focus find it difficult to focus on a task long enough to complete it. They are excessively distractible and struggle with blocking out background noise, background thoughts, and other environmental distractions. Others who struggle most in this area become hyper-focused on one thing and find it hard to pull their thoughts from that area. Having such a singular focus affects their class work, for despite exhortations to pay attention, they cannot seem to pull their thoughts from their video game or other compulsion. They have a difficult time selecting the most important thing to pay attention to.

Effort

You may be able to identify the students in your class who struggle with effort; they are the students who routinely fall asleep or seem drowsy in class. They have difficulty staying alert when they are not engaged in activities that provide motoric, social, or cognitive feedback.[28] These students are also sometimes sleepy due to the difficulty that they may have with falling asleep at night. While most teenagers have some sleep difficulties due to melatonin cycles, those with ADHD have more chronic or severe difficulties than their peers. In addition, this group of students may also work very slowly due to slow processing speeds. School assignments may take an inordinate amount of time, especially when the work requires both reading and writing. Due to their distractibility and a lack of alertness, students may have to re-read passages numerous times in order to gain any meaning.

Emotion

You will immediately know which students in your class with ADHD struggle with emotion. These students are the ones who fly off the handle at what seems like a moment's notice. They react quickly and often furiously when the other students push their buttons. They have a very low threshold for frustration and seem to have a very short fuse for outbursts of anger. They seem to become overwhelmed with the intensity of their feelings and often speak or act in ways that don't take into account others' feelings. These students often realize later that they have overreacted to slight criticisms and respond with feelings of sadness, discouragement, and depression.

Memory

Struggles with memory can significantly curtail the academic success of students with ADHD. Working memory is most significantly affected by ADHD, interfering with the student's ability to hold one bit of information while working with another.[29] Many aspects of academic work depend on working memory. In decoding words while reading, the student must hold onto all the letter sounds in order to put them together to make a word. Secondary students with ADHD often have even more difficulty in the area of reading comprehension. According to Brown, these students struggle with understanding the entire text even when they can decode every word.[30] Reading comprehension relies on working memory and sustained attention, working in concert to retrieve meaning from the text. If a student cannot attend to the text or hold the meaning of the text in working memory long enough to gain meaning from the text, he will find it difficult to answer questions or discuss the content of the text.

Math is another area in which working memory is essential. In order to complete most high-level math problems, students must manipulate many functions, using symbols and numbers in a fluid manner. The difficulty that some students with ADHD experience in sequencing operations makes algebra, geometry, and higher math nearly impossible.

Weaknesses in memory also affect students' ability to retrieve information at will. This type of memory weakness can have a significant impact on grades and academic success. When students cannot retrieve the information for the unit test or the final, they have no recourse but to receive failing grades. This difficulty in retrieving information from long-term memory for the task at hand creates a situation in which students give up and do not even try to study for tests. They realize that there is no consistent payoff for the effort they put into studying, given that there is no guarantee that they will be able to retrieve the necessary information at will. This abdication is often viewed as a lack of effort, but it is a learned response to many disappointing grades. Teachers need to consider allowing re-takes or open book or open note tests to support the needs of students with retrieval problems.

Action

Many students with ADHD struggle with monitoring and self-regulating their actions. These individuals tend to act without much forethought and are chronically restless and hyperactive. They find it difficult to slow down and inhibit their actions. Russell Barkley, a leading expert on ADHD, identifies the "impaired ability to inhibit" as the primary problem for these individuals.[31] The ability to monitor when it is best to act and when not to act significantly affects adolescents' social skills. In these situations, the young person has to monitor and regulate his actions while determining from the circumstances what expectations and perceptions that others have of him. He needs to recognize when it is appropriate to laugh at a joke and when it is not, when it is okay to make a joke and when it is not. Because individuals with ADHD have a hard time monitoring the context in which they are operating, they may report that they tend to be too random in what they notice, attending too much to some details and too little to others that may be equally or more important.[32] These types of individuals are the students who blurt out inappropriate things that come to mind without testing the waters to see whether they are appropriate. These students often find themselves in trouble for saying and doing things without even realizing what they did wrong.

Some students who struggle with executive functions in the area of self-regulating and monitoring may hyper-focus on others' reactions, making them excessively self-conscious. These students are very shy and inhibited in their social actions, always concerned about what others may think of them. They struggle with working in groups in the classroom; and without specific directions and responsibilities in a group, they will allow the others to take over and will participate as little as possible.

> Students who struggle with executive functions in the area of self-regulating and monitoring may hyper-focus on others' reactions, making them excessively self-conscious.

Students with ADHD have general difficulties with executive functions. Most will find that their ability to perform well in everyday tasks is affected by their difficulties with monitoring and self-regulating their actions. The lack of ability to inhibit their actions leads to many problems with other students, teachers, and others at school and at home. Their difficulties with monitoring themselves and the context they are in lead to problems with social situations, which in turn lead to a lack of friends and feelings of loneliness and depression. As one young woman with ADHD put it, "If you don't have any friends, what is the purpose of living?"

Other Disorders Associated with ADHD

From 50 to 90 percent of students with ADHD have associated disorders.[33] This fact alone should help teachers understand that no two students with ADHD will exhibit the same behaviors and academic weaknesses. In addition to learning disabilities, students with ADHD often exhibit other behavioral and mood disorders.[34]

Learning Disabilities

Experts estimate that between 10 percent and 50 percent of students with ADHD have learning disabilities. Typically, students with ADHD have the most difficulty with reading and written language as well as a high incidence of weaknesses in central auditory processing. Such students, who have average intelligence, struggle with grade-level tasks when the majority of the content is provided only through text-based constructs. Many of the strategies described in this book will address the specific needs of individuals with ADHD who also have learning disabilities.

Anxiety and Mood Disorders

As many as 25 percent of individuals with ADHD also suffer from anxiety disorders.[35] These are often related to school tasks such as test taking, navigating new social situations, and completing written assignments. In addition, many students with ADHD also have major depressive disorder or dysthymic disorder, which is chronic low-level depression and bipolar disorder. Young adults with these disorders complain of a loss of interest in activities and withdraw socially. They also may display severe irritability, defiance, and underachievement.[36] Young adults with bipolar disorder can swing quickly from the manic state, in which they feel happy, irritable, and restless to the depressive state, in which they experience feelings of sadness, hopelessness, and fatigue. Being informed about these mood disorders that can be associated with ADHD will help teachers recognize the patterns of these behaviors and be able to distinguish between behavior related to these disorders and willful behavior.

Oppositional Defiant Disorder and Conduct Disorder

Up to 60 percent of children and adolescents with ADHD have additional behavioral difficulties, which can include oppositional defiant disorder (ODD) and conduct disorder (CD).[37] Students diagnosed with ODD are often noncompliant and oppositional. They are often chronically negative, hostile, and defiant toward peers and authority figures. They are easily annoyed and have difficulty with accepting blame for their mistakes. Students with conduct disorder exhibit patterns of antisocial behavior and often violate the rights of others. They often bully, threaten, or try to intimidate others. Research strongly recommends early intervention and aggressive treatment of the underlying ADHD for these students. These most difficult-to-teach students will probably have specific behavior support plans in place to help address their behaviors and are likely to have a school counselor and a school psychologist managing their case. As the classroom teacher, it is essential that you have a clear understanding of the behavior support plan and the steps involved in proactively initiating and implementing the plan.

To Sum Up

Understanding ADHD and how it manifests in adolescents is essential for teachers who work with them. Recognizing that ADHD is not a willful choice but the result of neurological differences helps teachers to better understand the dilemmas that students with ADHD face. In addition, clearly understanding their struggle with executive functions and its effects on their academics, behavior, and social skills is significant. ADHD is a disability that is not simply about hyperactivity and having a hard time sitting still. For teachers and teaching professionals, it is of the utmost importance to recognize the broad, long-term effects of ADHD on every area of these young people's lives. It is within our power to stop the cycle of loneliness, anxiety, depression, and low self-esteem that result from misunderstood ADHD. Now we know, and now we can make a difference.

Chapter 3

Research-Based Teaching Strategies
Meeting the Needs of All Learners

Research everywhere points to the importance of instructional practices as a key to student academic success. Schools can use the best research-based materials and curricula, but no amount of research can guarantee student learning better than effective instruction. What makes good instruction, and how can it be measured? This is a question that is being asked nationally as schools try to determine what good teachers do that allows all students, including those with ADHD, to access the curriculum, learn the content, and master standards in the content areas.

Amid the hundreds of effective strategies, some of which will be highlighted in this chapter and throughout this book, the primary ingredient in student learning is effective student engagement. When students are active participants in learning rather than passive observers, true learning can occur.

> When students are active participants in learning rather than passive observers, true learning can occur.

The Engaging Classroom

As Chapter One mentions, active student engagement may require a paradigm shift for some who are used to the typical mode of lecture-based instruction. Effective instruction in a highly effective classroom is centered on student learning and academic results. Paula Rutherford, in her book *Instruction for All Students*,[1] compares the classroom of yesterday and the classroom of today:

Instruction Then	Instruction Now
Teacher-centered	Learner-centered
Organized around time	Organized for results
Single teaching strategy	Multiple teaching strategies
Teaching once	Re-teaching and enrichment
Whole-group instruction	Differentiated instruction
Passive learning	Active learning

This comparison makes it very clear that instruction now is focused on the needs of the learner. The practices involved are good news for students with ADHD, given their weaknesses in executive functions. The interaction provided in a modern classroom allows students with ADHD to maintain their focus, stay actively engaged, sustain their effort, and rely less on memorization and recall for success.

Focus on Student Learning

Effective teachers have a sound knowledge of the standards and the curriculum that must be taught. The process of identifying which standards and curriculum to teach will be discussed later in this chapter. The identification of what needs to be taught provides a more direct focus on instructional practices that will support students in meeting the standards. Creating this focus is essential, given that teachers are constantly faced with the dilemma of how to effectively spend the currency of education, which is time.[2] In light of this, teachers need to consider how each and every activity associated with a lesson is moving students toward meeting the standard. The fact that a lesson is in the textbook or has been the tradition of the school or grade level for eons is not a sufficient reason for students to do it.

Deep questions need to surround the decisions involved in instructional planning. The first focus must be on the standard that will be taught. How does this standard fit into the continuum of standards that will be addressed during the school year? Will upcoming assessments be aligned with this standard? How will you know that the standard has been met? What research-based instructional practices will support all students in meeting the standard? In addition, instructional planning teams, in light of the precious commodity of time, need to consider whether a lesson is worth the time it will cost to teach it and establish what is the most efficient way to teach the target standard.

When teachers use this process in their instructional planning, they will find that the burdens of trying to teach and use all the activities provided in the text fall away. They find that their goal is not to get through the textbook but rather to teach to the standard. When teaching teams identify the standards for each lesson, determine what resources are needed, what assessments or processes will determine mastery and how to differentiate to meet the needs of all students, the instructional planning process moves away from the daunting task of completing all the activities in the text and toward instruction that is focused sharply on student learning.

A focus on the standard is key when planning instruction and identifying the adaptations or accommodations necessary for a student with ADHD. When teachers focus on the standard and identify the objective or outcome of the lesson in concrete terms, often the activities that are not essential become more apparent. In an English class in which a student is writing a five-paragraph persuasive essay, the handwriting and the final form is not part of the standard being taught. This fact makes it clear that any student with ADHD who struggles with fine motor control need not be required to rewrite his essay in a final draft form unless the standard is about penmanship. If a student is able to produce the five paragraphs in a rough draft form, in a scaffolded sentence frame, using Inspiration software or a keyboarding device, it should be acceptable, because the standard is not about the handwriting but about the development of a five-paragraph essay.

Research-Based Strategies That Support Students with ADHD

Much has been written on instructional strategies that support the learning of each and every student. The seminal work of Robert Marzano, Deborah Pickering, and Jane Pollock was the first to look at specific instructional strategies; the authors applied research techniques to determine the effectiveness of the everyday strategies that effective teachers have used for some time.[3] Their book *Classroom Instruction That Works* has identified nine research-based strategies that are considered high-yield strategies in improving academic outcomes for students:

- Asking students to identify similarities and differences
- Teaching students to summarize and take notes
- Reinforcing effort and providing recognition
- Focusing on the important aspects of homework and practice
- Using nonlinguistic representations
- Facilitating cooperative learning
- Setting objectives and providing feedback
- Challenging students to generate and test hypotheses
- Using cues, questions, and advance organizers

The remainder of this section summarizes the instructional strategies advocated by Marzano, Pickering, and Pollock. Although these strategies were not specifically designed to meet the needs of students with ADHD, implementation of these strategies provides the type of instruction that meets the needs of students with attentional issues related to ADHD.

Asking Students to Identify Similarities and Differences

The ability to break a concept into its similar and dissimilar characteristics allows students to understand (and often solve) complex problems by analyzing them in a more concrete way. Students who are using this strategy analyze two or more elements in terms of their similarities and differences in one or more characteristics.[4] Figure 3.1 shows an example of how a Venn diagram can be used by students as a graphic organizer as they identify the similar and dissimilar characteristics of a topic. For students with ADHD, this strategy takes rote learning of facts, such as the underlying causes of the Civil War as in the figure, to a higher cognitive level of recognizing specific similarities and differences, allowing them to retain more information, stay more involved in thinking processes and thus be less likely to lose interest and become inattentive.

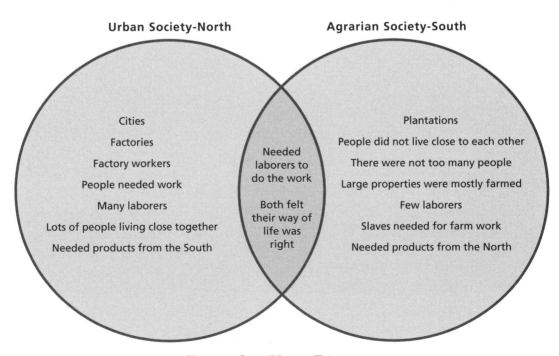

Figure 3.1: Venn Diagram

Strategies for Teaching Adolescents with ADHD

Teaching Students to Summarize and Take Notes

Teaching summarizing skills promotes greater comprehension by asking students to analyze information and determine the essential elements. Students delete non-essential information and then restate the most important elements in their own words in a summary form. The summarizing process is a difficult one, and students need to be clearly shown how to use their notes to write a summary. This process is discussed at greater length in the next chapter. Note taking requires students to determine which parts of the information are important and then record that information. As we know from Chapter Two, processing speed for students with ADHD is inhibited; therefore, note taking is a difficult and tedious task. Students need to be provided with graphic organizers that will help them chunk the information into meaningful parts. Using cloze notes, in which students fill in missing key information, or scaffolded Cornell notes will help students learn to identify essential elements and summarize key concepts. Figure 3.2 shows a simple note-taking scaffold that could be used to help students organize key concepts and questions.

Reinforcing Effort and Providing Recognition

All students respond when their efforts are recognized. Secondary school students with ADHD often have many negative school memories and are not accustomed

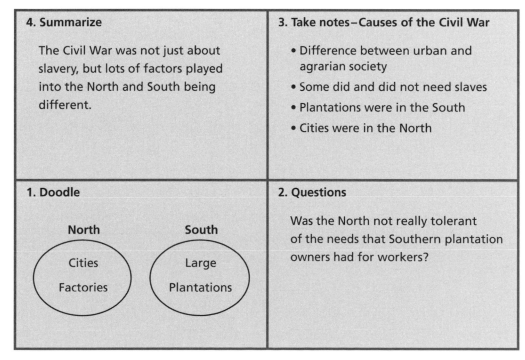

Figure 3.2: Note-Taking Scaffold

to receiving positive recognition. The strategy of recognizing students' efforts, when applied honestly, can be highly effective in motivating students with ADHD. Recognition of effort speaks loudly to the attitudes and beliefs of students. Recognizing achievement—any achievement—allows teachers to demonstrate the important connection between effort and achievement. Simply showing students that added effort does pay off in terms of improvement increases student achievement more than teaching them techniques for time management and comprehension of new material.[5] Praise, when it recognizes students for legitimate achievements, is extremely effective.

Focusing on the Important Aspects of Homework and Practice

Homework allows students to extend their learning outside the classroom but is often an area of extreme consternation for young adults with ADHD. It is usually necessary to allow accommodations or modifications of homework assignments for students with ADHD. Necessary adaptations necessary might include these:

- Ensure that students have a clear understanding of the task before they leave the classroom.

- Encourage students to work on homework together. Working with peers makes the work more doable and keeps students' attention.

- Allow modifications or adaptation in homework products, especially if the homework requires a lot of writing.

- Limit the number of skills practiced, to avoid confusing students.

- Limit the number of problems or tasks, given that it often takes students with ADHD a longer time to complete their work.

- Provide extra time for students to complete homework if assignments cannot be adapted or modified.

- Allow students to turn in homework electronically whenever possible. This option avoids lost papers and forgotten homework.

- Provide access to curricular content in a variety of ways, including electronic text, multimedia selections, and podcasts. Often, students with ADHD are digital natives and can relate to digital information with greater ease.

Research shows that the amount of homework assigned should vary by grade level and content area. Students with ADHD struggle significantly with homework, and its benefits should be weighed when you are making decisions about adaptations and accommodations pertaining to homework.[6] Homework can be an effective teaching tool, but its effectiveness is affected by the clarity of understanding on the part of the student about the purpose of the homework and how it relates to the content being learned as well as the timeliness and quality of feedback from the teacher.

Using Nonlinguistic Representations

Knowledge is stored in two forms: linguistic and visual. The use of visual scaffolds supports students who struggle with accessing their working memory and recalling information. Providing students with visual scaffolds to help them store knowledge creates greater opportunities for them to achieve. Instructional materials that have nonlinguistic components—for example, graphic organizers, pictures, multimedia, and video—provide concrete representations and mental images that improve learning by holding the attention of students with ADHD and by creating more meaningful contexts, facilitating greater retention in long-term memory. The use of graphic organizers to support memory of concepts will be discussed in more depth in the next chapter.

Facilitating Cooperative Learning

Organizing students into cooperative groups produces a positive effect on overall learning for all students but significantly supports the needs of students with ADHD. While students who struggle with inattention may fade in and out of listening to a typical informational lecture, grasping only parts of what has been said, participating in a group discussion promotes active participation by students with ADHD and does not allow long periods of inattention. When students are engaged in cooperative discussions, they are actively involved in the learning and find that they do not struggle with trying to keep their attention on the important information. Strategies that include specific expectations for each group member are the most effective, ensuring that all students participate and have a role to play.

Setting Objectives and Providing Feedback

Setting objectives is a powerful tool that provides students with specific information on the direction and outcome of each day's learning task. When objectives are written specifically enough, students very clearly understand their role in meeting the objective of each class and each lesson. With a clear and specific objective, the student with ADHD will not be lost or confused about what the expectations for that time period are. Setting objectives helps students to make connections between the classroom activities and what they are learning. Such connections create a context for the instruction and activities of each day, creating greater meaning that allows students with ADHD to stay actively involved and retain information in long-term memory.

Providing feedback is one of the most powerful research-based motivational strategies. In a recent review of education research, the Center on Instruction found that feedback is one of the top five most effective research-based instructional strategies.[7] Feedback is provided in a variety of ways; the most common form is grades, a form of feedback that rarely motivates a student with ADHD to make any academic changes. Grades are too static and often nebulous; they are not the type of feedback that the research literature advocates. Most students, especially those with ADHD, seldom see the connections between their class work, their effort, and the grades that they receive. Effective feedback is frequent and recognizes even the smallest of incremental improvements. Feedback techniques will be covered in more depth in Chapter Eight.

Challenging Students to Generate and Test Hypotheses

Students become actively involved when they are engaged in thinking. Having students apply their knowledge to either make predictions and prove them or take another's prediction or hypothesis and disprove it is a very effective way of challenging students to use high-level thinking skills and identify the learning strategies necessary to defend an answer or position. When students with ADHD are challenged in this manner, they find that they are engaged. This kind of active thinking and learning task is a far cry from ordinary boring school tasks, and it will hold the attention of students with ADHD.

Using Cues, Questions, and Advance Organizers

Using cues that hint at what is going to be taught, such as objects, pictures, or guiding questions, to begin a lesson is a very effective strategy for engaging the interest of students with ADHD. It also clues them in to what the lesson will be about and links the new topic to ones learned in the past. As I mentioned before, when tasks hold meaning, students with ADHD are more likely to remain engaged. Such activities help students to use what they already know about a topic to enhance further learning. Advance organizers help students to focus on what is important and are most effective when they are presented before a learning experience and then used throughout the process to guide a student in recognizing the important topics, key words, and essential content. Advance organizers are a very effective tool for students with ADHD who are easily overloaded by information coming at them or have difficulty distinguishing the important information from the unimportant. The advance organizer does this for them and thus proves to be one of the most effective academic tools for students with ADHD.

Meeting the Academic Challenges of Students with ADHD

Students with ADHD face numerous academic challenges that can be reduced in severity when teachers employ instructional approaches that meet the varied learning styles of the students in their classroom. Recognizing your own learning style and the differing styles of your students will make you a more effective teacher and lessen the challenges that your students with ADHD face every day.

Recognizing Different Learning Styles

Good teaching is not just about strategies. Teaching that is focused on students recognizes that different students learn differently and provides students with learning experiences that meet their learning needs. Most teachers teach in the modality that matches their strength and preferred learning style. For example, teachers who are auditory learners will use a lot of lectures; those who are visual learners will use a lot of visual tools like the overhead projector; and kinesthetic types are usually the most fun because they like to involve movement in their teaching. Traditionally, it has been the auditory, language-centered learner who ends up choosing teaching as a career, and our classrooms are filled with teachers who rely heavily on language and listening to obtain content knowledge.

As educators have come to recognize different types of learners through the early research on multiple intelligences by Howard Gardner and on learning styles by Rita Dunn and Kenneth Dunn, we can easily see that being able to identify learning styles and use them as a basis for instruction is vitally important for teachers in light of an increasingly diverse student population.[8,9] Here, I will briefly cover the three primary learning styles researched by Dunn and Dunn.

Visual Learners

Visual learners learn best from visual displays of information. Content for visual learners should be provided through visual materials such as pictures, charts, maps, diagrams, video clips, guided notes, handouts, and PowerPoint slides. You may find that these students like to take neat notes and highlight different sections in different colors. These students benefit from the liberal use of graphic organizers and are often seen doodling and drawing out ideas and concepts before beginning to write or answer questions. To support the needs of visually oriented students, allow them to sit toward the front of the room, where they can see the board or screen without obstructions and have a clear view of the teacher.

Auditory Learners

Auditory learners are logical, sequential thinkers. They like to talk about what they have learned, so they enjoy classroom discussions and debates. They like doing presentations and speeches and enjoy the opportunity to share their thoughts verbally. Auditory learners enjoy being read to and often subvocalize when they read in order to help themselves with comprehension. These students benefit from creating auditory mnemonics and like to create songs or jingles that will help them with memorization. Their needs can be met by allowing them to read out loud when they are working with new or difficult material and to use a recording device to help them with memory.

Tactile or Kinesthetic Learners

Tactile or kinesthetic learners are students who can see the whole picture. They are global thinkers. They can easily think outside the box and provide interesting and creative insights into the content being discussed. They also find it difficult to sit still for a very long time. They can learn new things while they move around, and you will often find them rocking in their seat or standing while reading or working. These students also highlight when they read and like to listen to music while studying and learning. They struggle with logical, analytical, or sequential tasks until they see the big picture, so they will often skim through the material to get a rough idea of what it is about before beginning to read or starting a project. To meet the needs of tactile or kinesthetic learners, allow them to move during instruction and give them chances to read, think, and share in creative ways.

Once teachers begin to realize that their classroom is filled with these diverse types of learners, it is easier to plan instruction that recognizes the needs of each group. Learning style inventories are available at *http://www.ldpride.net*.[10]

Differentiated Instruction: Principles of Universal Design for Learning

For teachers who struggle with identifying specific learning styles or modalities in their teaching, the principles of Universal Design for Learning (UDL), developed by the Center for Applied Special Technology, provide a more general framework that strives to facilitate instructional access for all types of learners, including those with ADHD. The center defines UDL as a framework for designing curricula that enables all individuals to gain access to knowledge in specific areas, practice grade-level skills, and maintain an enthusiasm for learning. To develop classroom instructional materials and practices that meet the UDL definition, they suggest that teachers follow the three principles of Universal Design:

1. **Use alternative formats to present information.** This principle includes the information on learning styles that was presented in the preceding section. This principle encourages teachers to focus on providing content instruction in a variety of formats that will meet the needs of students with different learning styles. This type of planning will help teachers ensure that they are enlisting the strengths of their auditory learners through the use of spoken word and text, visual learners through graphics and video, and kinesthetic learners through movement and hands-on activities.

2. **Provide alternative means of engagement.** This principle focuses on providing relevant, engaging instruction that allows learners to link new concepts to their own life or to prior learned knowledge. Such linkage creates a purpose or sets the stage for learning. Use of this principle removes the old structure of teaching fragmented pieces of information that are not grounded in any prior knowledge or real-life experience, a type of learning that is usually meaningless to students and very quickly forgotten. Alternative means of engagement include lessons that begin with video clips, relevant discussion, challenges that students must prove or disprove in the course of their learning, and links to prior knowledge or research.

3. **Provide alternative means for action and expression and assessment.** Teachers who use this principle realize that having students answer the questions at the end of a chapter in a textbook is only one way to assess students' knowledge. They realize that there are a variety of ways for students to show what they know, and they are willing to allow students to show their knowledge through writing, drawing, speaking, multimedia projects, or a combination of these forms. These teachers provide a menu of options that allows students to express their content knowledge in a way that best fits their learning style.[11]

Students with ADHD will find success when their teacher enlists strategies to meet the multimodal needs of all students. It is not the content that limits their learning; it is the manner in which the content is taught. With that in mind, let's look at how these strategies and concepts can be implemented in your classroom instruction.

> It is not the content that limits students' learning; it is the manner in which the content is taught.

Implementation of Instructional Strategies: Meeting the Needs of All Students Through Standards-Aligned Instruction

With knowledge of research-based instructional strategies and an understanding of learning styles and the principles of Universal Design for Learning, it is time to apply these concepts to instructional planning and delivery. When planning instruction, one must always go with the standards first. Many districts and even states have mandates about what constitutes the grade-level curriculum. Since the inception of NCLB, each state has been required to indentify standards that will be assessed. Much confusion about what constitutes a standard and how it should be taught has clouded teachers' staff rooms for the past decade. This section will help you clarify the importance of the standard and, even more important, your role in teaching that standard to *all* of your students.

Identifying Standards to Be Addressed

Although it is commonly believed that the curriculum *is* the textbook, the curriculum really is a structured set of learning outcomes for a prescribed course of study.[12] In many cases, the textbook does mirror the learning outcomes expected, but it alone is not the curriculum. This understanding on the part of teachers will clearly benefit secondary school students with ADHD. Whereas textbook teaching is often driven by lecture, reading, and note taking, standards teaching—deriving the prescribed course of study from standards rather than a textbook—can be provided through any manner of instruction. In essence, the standards determine the learning outcomes and the curriculum is the means through which that outcome is reached. Integral to success of any student in meeting the outcomes prescribed by the course of study is the manner in which the content is taught. Thus, instruction, the "how" we teach, is inextricably intertwined with the "what" of the curriculum. All students, including those with ADHD and other disabilities, need to learn what is in the curriculum; it is the instruction and the assessment methods that differ.

> Instruction, the "how" we teach, is inextricably intertwined with the "what" of the curriculum.

Ideally, the instruction part, the "how" we teach, is guided by research in the practices and strategies that are most effective. It behooves us as educators to embrace the strategies that are supported by research, to increase the opportunities for all students to have access to the curriculum. Coupled with effective instruction is the essential component of ongoing assessment *for* student learning in addition to assessment *of* student learning. It is essential that teachers grasp the new paradigm of ongoing assessment for learning—that is, assessing the effectiveness of their instruction on the content defined by the standards.

Planning Instruction to Meet the Standards

In today's standards-driven education environment, planning instruction to meet standards is essential. Teachers and schools have to ensure that the standards that are assessed in state accountability and federal accountability measures are taught. "What impact does this have on students with ADHD?" you may ask. The move toward curriculum planning and mapping to ensure that assessed standards are taught is changing the way teachers teach, and the change is in favor of students who have not been successful in accessing the curriculum through textbooks alone.

As teachers develop curriculum maps or pacing guides that are aligned to standards and benchmarks, they will find that textbooks do not always match the standards that are being assessed. They quickly realize that many of the lessons and activities that they have employed in the past have not been linked to any standard and do not facilitate any essential learning. Many times, teachers have found that these lessons ate up a lot of time but did not promote their students' progress in meeting the standards. In essence, teachers have found that they were wasting their own time and their students' precious instructional time on activities, lessons, and worksheets that were not even related to the standards. The time crunch necessary to teach a textbook from cover to cover is unnecessary. This realization has brought great relief to teachers and to their students, especially those who have a difficult time attending to tasks that do not have any evident purpose or meaning.

> Once lessons are standards-aligned, teachers quickly realize which activities do not facilitate essential learning.

Teaching to the standards has not always been embraced by teachers. Many teachers have perceived the standards movement as a form of Big Brother that has taken away their creativity. Once teachers understand clearly that the standards tell what to teach, not how to teach, they will find that standards-aligned instruction allows greater creativity and different models of learning. And the move away from textbook-based instruction will only help students with ADHD who have struggled with the traditional instructional practices.

Linking IEP Goals to Standards-Based Instruction

The move toward standards alignment has opened up a Pandora's box of questions about Individualized Education Plans (IEPs) under IDEA 2004 and students with disabilities, including those with ADHD significant enough to come under the "Other Health Impaired" (OHI) category.[13] Although past practice in regard to IEP goals has been to base the specially designed academic instruction of special education on a student's ability level, the standards movement and the state accountability of NCLB no longer allows this practice. Students are required to be assessed on grade-level standards; therefore, providing instruction that does not include grade-level standards is inappropriate except for those students with the most significant cognitive impairments. While separate remedial instruction has been the norm in special education, this practice will no longer be acceptable if students are expected to meet grade-level benchmarks on statewide assessments.

The change to grade-level assessment for all students has created a paradigm shift in the way that special education services are provided. More and more special education students are receiving their core content instruction in the general education setting, with collaborative support from special education personnel. The positive outcome of these collaborative models is that general education teachers who teach core content are learning important instructional strategies from the special education experts, allowing them to design instruction that better meets all of their students' varied needs.

Special education support has moved out of the trailer and into the general education classroom. In order for a general education teacher to provide instruction that meets IEP goals, the goals must be written in a congruent manner—that is, they must require grade-level instruction in grade-level content, so that the general education teacher routinely, within the scope of the grade-level instruction, meets the goals. This focus on grade-level content for students identified with ADHD under the OHI category ensures that they are not detoured onto a path of lowered expectations and inferior outcomes. Ultimately, in a collaborative model in which special education strategy experts team with classroom teachers of core content, all students, including those with ADHD, benefit. The classroom teacher moves from being a teacher of content to being a teacher of students.

Connecting the Lesson to the Standard

When teaching teams and schools have developed curriculum maps linked to their standards, instructional planning becomes much more strategic. Instead of following the pacing guides developed by textbook publishers and teaching the lessons as they fall, teachers make their own decisions about what lessons best meet the needs of their own students and ensure that their students are learning the content of the standard. When teachers clearly understand the standard that is being taught in a lesson and when they clearly communicate that standard or objective, students with ADHD have a clearer understanding of the expectations for each period of the day. When daily expectations are unclear and the instruction is not relevant or related to any standard or objective, students with ADHD struggle with focusing their time and creative energy on something that seems pointless. This behavior is most often perceived as disinterest and a lack of work ethic. Students tend to see unfocused lesson activities as busywork and find it difficult to focus their attention on work that has no interest, no meaning, and no purpose. Most often, the result is a student who simply does not do the work or turns in work that is very poorly done.

Providing the standard or objective for each lesson taught can change students from passive to active learners. Madeline C. Hunter points out that students usually extend more effort and, consequently, increase their learning if they know what they will be learning.[14] An objective that specifically identifies what the student will have accomplished by the end of the period makes it very clear that the student will be *doing something*. The student cannot take a passive stance in relation to the daily instruction. The student can see clearly where the lesson is going and how she will interact with the lesson. When an objective specifically states, for example, "Students will identify six instances of figurative language in the story *Camp Harmony* and write these in their lab books," there is no question as to what the student will need to do before she leaves the room.

> When an objective specifically states, for example, "Students will identify six instances of figurative language in the story *Camp Harmony* and write these in their lab books," there is no question as to what the student will need to do before she leaves the room.

This kind of specific direction is very beneficial to students with ADHD, who may struggle more in an environment in which the outcome and the purpose for the instruction is unclear. When a student sees a direct correlation between the objective and the activities of the lesson, he is more likely to complete the activity, improving his grades and his own perception of himself as a student.

When the objective is posted in the classroom for each period, students have a very clear understanding of your expectations for their instructional time in your classroom. Teachers have also commented that having the standard posted helps them to maintain a focus on the standard during their instruction and does not allow them to "rabbit trail" off on a tangent. The standard posted in the classroom helps both the students and the teacher stay focused. In addition to focusing the actual delivery of instruction on the standard, identifying the standard during planning helps the teacher quickly realize which actions or activities in the lesson are actually for the purpose of teaching the standard. They find at this point that many busywork activities are no longer necessary.

Determining whether students have met the standard is another standards-aligned instructional decision that grade-level or content teaching teams need to make. Having rubrics for what constitutes proficiency or below proficiency is helpful for the teacher in determining when it is time to move on or time to re-teach and is also helpful for students in determining whether they have met the standard when doing independent work. Providing students with exemplars of proficient work and below-proficient work helps them have a clearer understanding of what is expected of them. These models are very helpful for students with ADHD in learning to become responsible for their own learning and performance. If they have a clear model of what an "A" paper looks like, they are likely to use that understanding to help them improve their own work. If the concept of an "A" paper is nebulous, they are less likely to be able to figure out what they need to do in order to attain that level of proficiency.

Instructional Design That Supports Students with ADHD

All students benefit from instructional practices developed through thoughtful instructional planning. Teachers who regularly take the time to plan their instruction with the needs of their students with ADHD in mind make it possible for their students to routinely experience more academic success. When you implement instructional practices that recognize the importance of consistent rituals and routines and ongoing instructional scaffolding, you will find that your students with ADHD will be able to complete instructional tasks as successfully as their peers.

Rituals and Routines

In addition to providing students with the support of clearly defined standards and objectives for each lesson taught, it is also important to establish a set of schoolwide classroom rituals and routines. These will be discussed further in Chapter Seven, but it is essential to include this concept when discussing daily instructional expectations.

The rituals and routines of your classroom should include such things as routine entry procedures that often include a warm-up, so that students are engaged as soon as they enter the room. "Ritualized" classrooms have routines for how to walk in, how to turn in homework, how to head a paper, how to ask for help, and how to respond to questions. In this type of classroom, a student with ADHD is supported by a teacher who posts the daily agenda, the objective, homework assignments, and any materials needed for the lesson in the same place every day. A student with ADHD, who may lose focus for some time during class, can always be reassured that she can look at the agenda to figure out where the class is, at the objective to tell her what they are working on, and to the routines to know what will happen next.

Instructional Scaffolding

All students benefit from instructional scaffolding, but students with ADHD and concomitant learning disabilities cannot survive without it. These students need more than simple modeling and cannot be expected to move on to independent practice after a short introduction provided by the teacher. Instructional scaffolding needs to be provided on an ongoing basis, until, through frequent checks for understanding, the teacher is sure that 95 percent of the class is able to do the independent practice successfully. Anita Archer, a well-known speaker and author on instructional strategies and scaffolds, makes very clear that teachers need to do many repetitions of "I do, I do, I do" and "we do, we do, we do, we do, we do, we do" before they can ever expect students to do a "you do" on their own (see Figure 3.3).[15] Students with ADHD need this additional scaffolded support to help them clearly understand what they are supposed to do.

In addition to many opportunities to practice before he is expected to do his own independent practice, a student with ADHD may still need the support

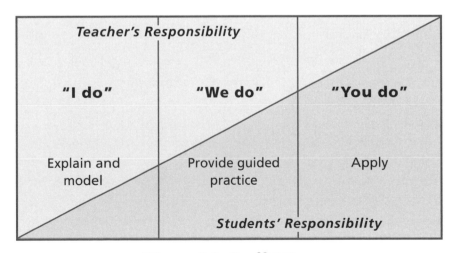

Figure 3.3: Scaffolding

Source: Huck Fitterer, WestEd Teach4Success Project. Adapted and used with permission.

of models and exemplars of exactly what is expected of him. The teacher often models on the overhead or the whiteboard, but unfortunately, when students are expected to complete the independent practice part, often the overhead is turned off or the board is erased. Students with ADHD (and many others) may need the model to remain in place so that they can reconstruct the steps necessary to complete the assignment. For more difficult assignments like reports, written papers, or written responses, these students need to see examples of different levels of proficiency, so that when they need to revise or improve their work, they have an idea of what is involved and have a clear example to work toward.

Checking for Understanding

How does a teacher know that a majority of his students are ready to move on to independent practice? How does he know that a student with ADHD is ready to work independently or complete an assignment at home? This can only occur if the teacher frequently checks for understanding throughout all the stages of a lesson.

Checking for understanding does not mean that a teacher asks, "Does anyone have any questions?" As most teachers know, this response usually elicits very few responses, and the poor student who does ask a question usually gets groans and negative feedback from her peers. This is a completely ineffective way to check for understanding. Students with ADHD will not identify themselves as needing help in front of the whole class, and neither will most secondary school students. Teachers need to enlist other strategies that will allow them to know when students are ready to move to the "you do" stage.

Checking for understanding can be done in a variety of ways. One very easy approach to assessing whether all students are ready to move on is the use of small whiteboards. This tool helps teachers to very quickly assess whether most of the students in the class have grasped the concept as well as which students have not. Asking or posting a simple question or problem and having students write the response on their whiteboard allows the teacher to see who does and does not have it. This is impossible to do when students are doing their practice on paper, because the teacher cannot move around the room quickly enough to see all student papers. Having the whiteboards held up gives a teacher the snapshot that he needs in order to recognize who does and does not have the concept.

In addition to whiteboards, teachers can use a variety of response cards to respond to questions. These are best used for yes-or-no and multiple-choice questions; students hold up a card to respond "yes" or "no" or hold up a color card, number card, or letter card that serves as a response to a multiple-choice or true-or-false question. Teachers can also check for understanding by having students use hand gestures. A simple thumbs up or thumbs down is one way to gather responses to a true-or-false question or to have students respond to a question about how well they understand a concept. Thumbs up signals confidence to move on; a thumb sideways indicates a bit of uncertainty; and thumbs down indicates a need for further clarification or re-teaching. For multiple-choice responses, students can simply hold up the number of fingers that corresponds with the correct answer in the answer series.

These strategies for checking for understanding require constant and active participation on the part of students. This type of instructional strategy does not allow a student with ADHD to let his mind wander or to spend much time off task. The fact that all students are required and expected to respond with a whiteboard, response card, or gesture keeps all students participating and actively engaged. When engaged, the student with ADHD will find it easier to maintain focus and participate with greater frequency and success.

Independent Practice

Once a teacher is aware, through frequent checks for understanding, that students are ready, it is time to move into independent practice, the part of the lesson that allows students to develop the skills necessary to demonstrate mastery of the standard on their own. Students with ADHD need limited time for independent practice in the classroom. Students who struggle with focused attention, even when they have the skill to complete the work, will struggle with completion when too much time is dedicated to this part of the lesson. Lack of focus, lack of ability to attend for long periods of time, and the inability to sit and work quietly for extended periods make this part of a lesson very hard for these students. In addition to lack of attention, lack of clarity on how to move ahead will often impede a student from moving forward and doing anything. To alleviate these problems, teachers can use the following strategies:

- Write abbreviated directions on the board. These directions can be three- or four-word bulleted phrases.

- Highlight important steps. Key words can be highlighted with a highlighter or underlined on the overhead transparency to support key ideas. These key words can make up the abbreviated directions.

- Have students talk about what the directions say. Often just talking about it clarifies confusion.

To keep students working:

- Have students make a quick list, on their own, of the directions and tasks required. Encourage them to check off the tasks or cross them off as they complete them.

- Have students write steps on sticky notes and then remove the notes as tasks are completed.

- Allow students to give abbreviated answers or respond electronically rather than on paper.
- Allow students to work with a partner to complete the task, and give a shared grade.

Homework is another form of independent practice. This chapter has already discussed some of the issues related to homework. When making homework decisions, it is important to remember some of the following strategies and adaptations:

- Adjusting the length of the assignment
- Helping students to connect with a study group
- Helping students access after-school programs
- Providing technological support such as computers and calculators
- Checking frequently with students about assignments, and helping them break large assignments into chunks
- Allowing alternate response formats like oral reports, posters, PowerPoint presentations, or graphic displays

To Sum Up

Good teaching supports the needs of all students. The research-based strategies and the standards-aligned instruction discussed in this chapter will allow all the students in your classroom to be successful. As an educator, you will find that once these strategies are successfully employed, teaching is once again an exciting, creative, and invigorating practice. Keeping students with ADHD actively engaged in learning is how you, the content expert, can provide them with the best and most successful access to the curriculum possible.

Chapter 4

Strategies to Support Students with ADHD in English Language Arts

The preceding chapter discussed specific teaching strategies that teachers can use in teaching any type of content in their classrooms. This chapter and the next two chapters will focus on instructional practices in specific content areas as well as how some of the strategies that were previously discussed can be applied to each content area.

If you peruse this chapter quickly, you will see that it is not full of typical lesson plans modeled on a Madeline Hunter lesson design. Most teachers have had this kind of pre-service training on how to design a teacher-led lesson of the kind commonly found in teacher's editions of textbooks. In this chapter, we will look at a research-based model of instruction that supports the needs of all students and, specifically, the needs of students with ADHD. This chapter will briefly describe the learner-centered classroom, which differs considerably from the content-centered classroom.

The Learner-Centered Classroom

The learner-centered classroom focuses on the student and learning rather than on the adult and teaching. This is a major paradigm shift from the teacher as "sage on the stage" to the teacher as a facilitator of learning opportunities in

> The learner-centered classroom focuses on the student and learning rather than on the adult and teaching.

which the students do the talking and the work. Despite the research supporting these practices, teachers have been initially reluctant to embrace this model for a variety of reasons. The primary concerns have been about classroom management. Teachers have been concerned that if students are allowed to talk to each other, they will get off topic and not get through the lesson for the day or that if strict quiet is not kept, students will get out of control and the teacher will not be able to bring the students back together as needed. In addition, many teachers in specific content areas see themselves as teachers of content and not specifically as teachers of students. In their minds, they teach the content, often in the "stand and deliver" mode, and if students do not learn the content, it is the students' fault.

Fortunately for all students, but especially for students with ADHD and other learning disabilities, these days are coming to an end. As the focus on teaching changes from grades to student learning, the delivery of classroom instruction will change for the better. Student-centered learning is about firsthand learning, group learning, practicing, reflecting, teaching of others, and presentations because all of these activities require active engagement of the learner.[1] Research shows that when students are actively engaged in learning, the dendrites—the connective pathways in the brain—grow.[2]

Developing Collaboration Skills

Using learner-centered instructional approaches is effective not only for supporting the development of content learning but, more importantly, for developing in your students the attitudes, behaviors, learning skills, and critical thinking skills necessary for a successful career. Students working in small groups not only achieve deeper levels of thinking but also develop the important communication skills of talking with and listening to others. Having students frequently do classroom presentations allows them to practice skills that are essential to most careers. In the learning-centered classroom, content knowledge and effective collaboration skills rather than grades become the focus of instruction.

We cannot expect students to have the necessary skills for learner-centered approaches, so it is important to realize that students will need to be directly taught many of the skills needed to embrace this type of instruction. Some students who are very comfortable being passive learners will find this type of instruction uncomfortable and challenging. These students have become accustomed to an approach in which the teacher does all the work and the student simply responds by performing tasks that the teacher has developed. Often, these tasks require only the lowest level of cognition—the basic recall level—and students can easily float through each day without ever really taxing their brain or coming up against any learning challenges.

Taking Ownership of Learning

A student-centered classroom requires students to take ownership of their own learning. They learn to ask themselves questions related to the content and figure out how and where to find the answers. This skill is very different from memorizing notes and answering questions out of the textbook. Students also learn how to communicate with each other, share workloads, and teach each other in cooperative learning groups and small learning communities. These methods are in contrast to the independent practice that is common in most classrooms, in which students are expected to finish tasks without any outside discussion; outside discussion or collaboration is viewed as cheating and is frowned upon. In a student-centered classroom, students become effective speakers and communicators by making presentations in front of their peers and learn how to evaluate themselves and their work through the effective use of rubrics and exemplars.

> Collaboration on learning and assignments creates an environment in which the student can use her strengths and can become a powerfully contributing member of a group. In contrast, if such a student were left to navigate the traditional "read-and-regurgitate" model, she would be much more likely to fail.

A learning-centered classroom is a place where secondary school students with ADHD can shine. Collaboration on learning and assignments creates an environment in which the student can use her strengths and become a powerfully contributing member of a group. In contrast, if such a student were left to navigate the traditional read-and-regurgitate model, she would be much more likely to fail.

The learning-centered classroom is a noisy, active, energizing place of discovery and learning. Let's look at some ways that classroom instruction within the learning-centered model can make the content a meaningful, powerful learning tool for all students.

Teaching English Language Arts

Instilling a love for reading and literature is the goal of most language arts teachers. Having opportunities to read and engage in conversations about the classics is not just essential for passing high school, but is also part of the bigger picture of creating well-rounded, knowledgeable adults. Although the ninth graders in your classroom may not see reading William Golding's *Lord of the Flies* or George Orwell's *1984* as very meaningful to them right now, little do they know that they may someday hear these classics mentioned in a conversation and will have the distinct privilege of actively participating in the conversation. It is hard for them to see that these classics teach important life and social lessons, but at this point, students, especially students with ADHD, find working toward ambiguous, "sometime in the future" goals difficult. It is the role of the English language arts teacher to bring these classics to life for all of her students, including those with ADHD. In addition to teaching the core messages and themes of the classics, English language arts teachers also hold the responsibility of teaching students to meet the standards in literary analysis as well as vocabulary and written language content and conventions. When teachers take these tasks and provide instruction in a student-centered manner, students will find pleasure in these classics, become competent in meeting the English language arts standards, and be able to express what they know in writing.

The Research

In response to the National Assessment of Educational Progress data from 2007, which showed that 69 percent of eighth graders fall below the proficient level in their ability to comprehend the meaning of a text at their grade level, the research study from the Institute of Education Sciences called *Improving Adolescent Literacy* makes the following recommendations:

- Provide explicit vocabulary instruction.
- Provide direct and explicit instruction in comprehension strategies.
- Increase student motivation and engagement in literacy learning.
- Make available intensive interventions for struggling readers.[3]

In addition, the Center on Instruction has developed *Effective Instruction for Adolescent Struggling Readers: A Practice Brief*.[4] Although there has been much research on early literacy and the prevention of reading failure, little research has been done on meeting the needs of adolescents who struggle with reading. The authors identify the need for effective practices in literacy instruction for adolescents because so many struggling readers fail to understand what they read. Older students are tackling complex informational texts and are facing serious and growing challenges in content areas. Efficient literacy skills are a necessity in order for students to be successful in the content areas. Even in our modern multimedia world, after third grade, most knowledge in content areas is presented through print-based resources.[5] This fact makes it essential that all students have adequate literacy skills in order to be successful in the content areas. The instructional recommendations made by Alison Gould Boardman and her colleagues include literacy instruction organized into five general categories:

- Word study
- Fluency
- Vocabulary
- Comprehension
- Motivation[6]

In looking at the recommendations of these two studies, the common practices that will help all students become successful readers are revealed. We will look at each of these important areas in more depth and will identify how the recommended strategies can help the students in your classroom.

Institute of Education Sciences	Center on Instruction
Explicit vocabulary instruction	Vocabulary
Direct and explicit instruction in comprehension strategies	Comprehension
Motivation and engagement in literacy learning	Motivation
Intensive individualized interventions	Word study
	Fluency

The Practice

Much of the research on adolescent literacy focuses on the vocabulary deficit of many young people today. Identifying specific instructional practices that will close the vocabulary gap is the focus of effective research-based instructional practice. It is not enough to give your students a vocabulary list for the week to memorize and expect that this practice will increase their working vocabulary. Recognizing the need for explicit vocabulary instruction, prioritizing subject-specific words, and providing instruction on the academic vocabulary necessary to access the content instruction are essential to effective reading instruction.

Students with ADHD struggle significantly with reading comprehension for a variety of reasons. While strategies to improve reading comprehension continue to focus on active reading strategies, recent research supports the use of explicit comprehension instruction. The research-based practices of using advance organizers, graphic organizers, and self-monitoring allow dynamic involvement with the text, which helps students with ADHD stay actively engaged in the reading process. Extended discussion offers them additional opportunities to interact with the text in meaningful ways.

Writing is a challenge for students with ADHD. While the research completed by the Institute of Education Sciences and the Center on Instruction did not focus specifically on writing, as a teacher of secondary students, you have probably recognized the need for explicit writing instruction for your students with ADHD. The organizational task of developing a written product is daunting to a student with ADHD. Practices that make this daunting task doable through self-regulation strategies will provide students with ADHD with avenues for tackling their writing challenges.

Explicit Vocabulary Instruction

In a society that relies heavily on visual stimuli for entertainment and learning, most students in classrooms today have vocabulary deficits. The lack of time spent reading exacerbates the problem. Overcoming these deficits needs to be the focus of all instruction and must be intentional. Knowing word meaning is essential for comprehension and overall academic success; therefore, explicit instructional support needs to be provided to ensure that all students have the opportunity to acquire the necessary vocabulary for academic success.[7]

Explicit instructional strategies for increasing vocabulary vary, but they consist primarily of direct instruction on word meaning and instruction that supports independent vocabulary acquisition skills. Direct instruction on word meaning can include common topics such as using dictionaries and glossaries, using context clues to derive meaning, and using graphic displays of the relationships among words and concepts such as semantic maps. Effective vocabulary instruction engages students in developing "word consciousness," in which a student understands not just one meaning of a word in a single context but the varied use of a word in different language contexts.[8] According to Michael F. Graves, getting students to this level of word knowledge requires explicit instruction that focuses on three areas:

> Effective vocabulary instruction engages students in developing "word consciousness."

1. **Additive vocabulary instruction,** which focuses on teaching specific words

2. **Generative vocabulary instruction,** which teaches word-learning strategies

3. **Academic vocabulary instruction,** which addresses word learning and word-learning strategies in specific academic content areas[9]

Additive Vocabulary Instruction

Additive vocabulary instruction focuses on words that are important and useful for students to know. Isabel Beck, Margaret McKeown, and Linda Kucan,[10] who are experts on vocabulary instruction, identify three tiers of vocabulary instruction:

Tier 1 words are words that the student is likely to know. These are not words that need any focused instructional time.

Tier 2 words are words that appear frequently in different contexts. Beck and her colleagues suggest that teachers focus vocabulary instruction on these words.

Tier 3 words rarely appear in text, but they are essential to learning specific content. Because these words are essential to knowledge in content areas, teachers have to balance instruction between Tier 2 and Tier 3. As teachers are deciding which Tier 3 words to focus on, they should determine their frequency of use and ensure that students have strong knowledge of the foundational words for relevant areas of study. For words that are not foundational words, vocabulary instruction is important, but a personal glossary or a classroom word wall of words and meanings can be a useful tool, especially for students with ADHD who struggle with retrieval.

Specific vocabulary instruction should be engaging to students and should go well beyond looking up words in a dictionary and copying their definition. This activity is useless if students do not actively engage in understanding the meaning of the words they are copying! Students should be involved in creating their own definitions and nondefinitions, drawing pictures, using graphic organizers, and playing word games, allowing them to practice using the new words. Figure 4.1 shows a graphic organizer developed by Kate Kinsella that provides spaces for students to write definitions in their own words and to brainstorm different ways that the word may be used. The Frayer model (Figure 4.2) is a useful graphic organizer for word analysis; it requires students to define the term, describe its essential characteristics, and then provide both examples and non-examples in a manner similar to the Kinsella model. Both of these graphic organizers cause the student to think of word meaning and determine characteristics of the word either verbally or visually, and then apply the information by thinking of examples or non-examples.

Generative Vocabulary Instruction

Strategies that promote independent vocabulary acquisition skills include analyzing words and their parts in context to derive meaning based on prior knowledge and the context in which the word is presented. This approach allows students to generalize the skills learned in direct instruction and expand their vocabulary knowledge in a variety of texts in multiple contexts. Generalized vocabulary instruction capitalizes on the relatedness of words and classes of words.[11] Students learn the meanings of new words based on their existing knowledge of words and word parts. The graphic organizer in Figure 4.3 creates the structure for learning the meaning of a new word as a specific part of speech.

Word	Meaning	Example	Practice
lexicon **lex•i•con** (noun)	1. All the words in a language	The modern English lexicon The ancient Greek lexicon	The English lexicon has added many new words recently from the _____ industry.
(noun)	2. The special vocabulary of a profession or hobby	Doctors use a medical lexicon that includes special words to describe symptoms like idiopathic.	Skaters use a lexicon with words like _____ to refer to _____. Baristas use a lexicon with words like _____ to refer to _____.

Figure 4.1: Kinsella's Graphic Organizer

Source: Kate Kinsella. Used with permission.

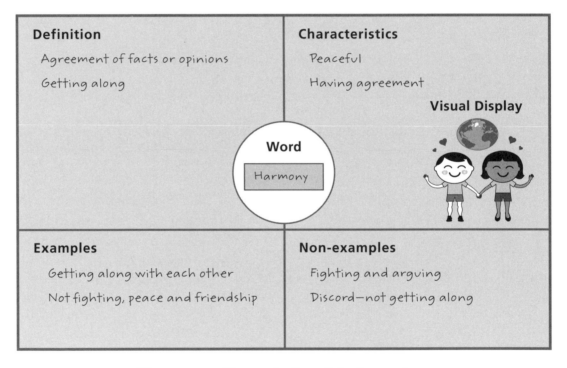

Figure 4.2: Frayer's Graphic Organizer

Source: Frayer, Frederick, & Klausmeier, 1969.

Academic Vocabulary Instruction

Students need to understand the vocabulary that is related to the concepts that they are learning. They also need to learn the key terms or academic vocabulary that is essential in order to navigate the instruction related to the content. For example, if students are not aware of what the term *figurative language* means, they will find it very difficult to identify it in the text. Beyond word acquisition related

Strategies for Teaching Adolescents with ADHD

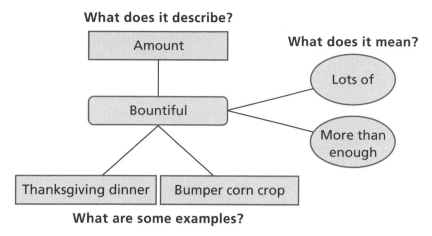

Figure 4.3: Adjective Map

to the content that students are learning, rich discussion of academic vocabulary is also essential. Discussion benefits learners in that they are able to participate as both speakers and listeners. If the teacher has planned carefully for the acquisition of academic vocabulary, students are provided with numerous opportunities to use new words in discussion as well as gain a clearer understanding of the vocabulary from the insights of their peers.

To ensure that students have the learning experiences they need to close the vocabulary deficit, teachers must dedicate a portion of each class period exclusively to vocabulary instruction. Repeated exposure to vocabulary words can occur only if students are given a chance to speak, discuss, and study the words in context. Providing students with strategies to derive meaning from word study in context is also another powerful way to improve vocabulary knowledge that will benefit all students. This process will be discussed further when we present intensive interventions later in this chapter.

While students learn from explicit vocabulary instruction and many opportunities to practice using the vocabulary, we also know that students' comprehension of new concepts and word meanings are supported by the use of visual media. Obtaining pictures, videos, and other images to help students conceptualize word meanings is the most effective strategy for many learners, including many of those with ADHD.

Explicit Instruction in Comprehension Strategies

All students must develop routines and procedures that help them make sense of texts. Due to weaknesses in executive functions, students with ADHD do not always develop sequential routines that allow them to derive meaning from a text. They struggle with remembering what has been read. For this reason, explicit

> Explicit comprehension strategies must be taught that will support or scaffold the development of routines for deriving meaning from a text for the student with ADHD.

comprehension strategies must be taught that will support or scaffold these processes for the student with ADHD. In order for the written material to hold meaning, the student must be given a chance to actively participate in the process. Sitting and listening to others read or even trying to read silently is a passive process that will not hold the attention of students with ADHD.

Activating Prior Knowledge

Activating prior knowledge is one strategy that helps students who struggle with reading to make connections from what they already know to what they are learning. This process brings the reader into the context of what they will be reading. Students with ADHD need specific strategies that invite them to activate prior knowledge. Such strategies include teaching students how to preview headings in the text, make predictions, or identify key concepts *before* reading.

Using Graphic Organizers

Graphic organizers allow these students to identify, organize, and remember important ideas that they read. Examples of graphic organizers include story maps, which identify characters, setting, and plot; framed outlines, which help the student identify the main details related to a topic by answering specific questions; concept maps, which record the essential concepts of a topic, helping the student identify what the concept is, what it is like, and some examples (see Figure 4.4); and Venn diagrams, which help students identify similarities and differences between topics. Explicitly teaching students with ADHD how to use graphic organizers is essential in helping them to comprehend the content and access the core materials in their textbooks.

Summarizing

In order for students with ADHD to be actively involved in comprehension, they must be shown how to summarize main ideas, ask themselves questions, paraphrase what has been read, discuss the content, draw inferences, and frequently stop, ask, discuss, and answer questions *while* reading. Framed outlines, graphic organizers that support topic summaries, and the ongoing identification of key points in graphic organizers or notes help students to remember and recognize the main points so that they can organize them into effective summaries. This is a difficult area for students with ADHD, and they may need ongoing support or scaffolding in order to learn how to delete the unimportant information and

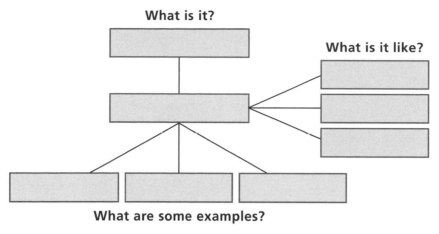

What is it?

What is it like?

What are some examples?

Figure 4.4: Concept Map

identify the salient information in their notes. Teacher modeling is the best way to teach students with ADHD this difficult task.

Self-Monitoring

Beyond using graphic organizers to help them organize their thinking about what they have read, students with ADHD need to be taught strategies that will help them recognize when comprehension has broken down. These comprehension monitoring strategies enable students to keep track of their understanding as they read and to implement "fix-up" strategies when understanding breaks down.[12] Although all of us wander off in our thinking when we are reading, we realize it more quickly than students with ADHD and we usually fix the problem by re-reading from where we began to lose meaning. Struggling readers, including those with ADHD, often do not do this. They must be directly taught strategies to monitor their comprehension because their weaknesses in self-regulation and monitoring often prevent them from recognizing when they have gotten off track.

The strategies suggested by Boardman and her colleagues for this self-monitoring process include teaching students to recognize when their understanding is breaking down (for example, by noting confusing words or concepts while they are reading), to draw images to help them remember concepts as they read, or to stop after each paragraph to summarize or generate questions.[13] They also suggest teaching students to use fix-up strategies such as re-reading, restating, or using other strategies to determine the meaning of confusing words. In addition, comprehension can be monitored by getting students actively involved in comprehension strategies—for example, questioning, guided notes, or confirming or disconfirming predictions—as they read.

Discussing Text Meaning and Interpretation

The most important goal of literacy instruction is to increase the comprehension of complex text.[14] To accomplish this goal, teachers must engage their students in high-quality discussions of the meaning and interpretation of the text. Students must have a chance to have sustained exchanges with the teacher and with other students in which they can defend their interpretations, viewpoints, and reasoning based on the text. Only through frequent discussions can students develop and use the skills of creating interpretations, using background knowledge, reasoning to support their interpretations and conclusions, and listening to the points of view and arguments of others. In a learning-centered language arts classroom, the instructional goal is not about grades but about developing these essential skills in comprehending text.

> Teachers must engage their students in high-quality discussions of the meaning and interpretation of the text.

> Social collaboration on reading and reading-related tasks motivates students with ADHD to persist and continue working.

Allowing reluctant readers to collaborate by reading together, sharing their ideas, and explaining and presenting their knowledge increases their motivation to read. Research by John Guthrie and Nicole Humenick showed that when students collaborate socially on reading and reading-related tasks, they find their work more motivating and often continue working even after completing the assigned task.[15] Creating such collaborative opportunities takes careful planning on the part of the teacher, and for some teachers, it creates apprehension about classroom management and keeping discussions on task.

In a learning-centered classroom in which discussion is well planned, inappropriate discussion is the exception and not the norm. The planning for extensive discussion must include selections that are engaging to the student and describing situations or contexts that can have multiple interpretations. Creating numerous brief opportunities to discuss and analyze is an effective strategy for keeping discussions centered on content. Preparing questions for discussion that stimulate students to think reflectively, forcing them to make high-level connections, teaches students how to construct meaning even from difficult text. Questions that guide the discussion, along with frequent checks for understanding or check-ins with the group as a whole, facilitate effective and extended discussion that improves comprehension and critical thinking skills.

While teachers may be concerned about their students' ability to stay focused on the discussion, especially those with ADHD, several strategies can provide both the teacher and the students with specific structures that support focused, productive discussions.

Provide tasks for each discussion member, so that each member has a specific job and a specific responsibility. When expectations for the discussion are clear and each person has an assignment, there is less of a chance for one or two persons to monopolize the conversation or for a few people to let the others do all the work.

Develop, practice, and use a specific protocol or set of questions to guide each discussion. This type of structure and routine is a good way to help reluctant participants to become comfortable with the discussion format. Guiding questions can be as concrete as these:

- Explain your position on the topic.
- Defend your position with three examples.
- Provide one arguable point.
- Defend your position against the argument.

When teachers consistently use this format for guided discussion, students with ADHD become familiar with the expectations, and when expectations are clear, students have more success in staying focused and complying with teacher directives.

Whenever students are working in discussion groups, it is imperative that the teacher actively circulate around the room and among the groups to redirect discussions that have gone off topic, to model thinking strategies, or to ask additional questions that will push students to discuss and think at deeper levels.

Students who do not participate much in whole-class discussions, spending most of their instructional time as passive learners, often find that interaction in the discussions is rewarding and engaging enough to bring them into active learning. Students who may have disliked language arts in the past are now actively participating, and through this participation, they are learning the concepts of literary analysis and other important literacy skills but also learning how to defend their own thinking and how to accept diverse viewpoints as they think more deeply about what they are reading.

Motivation and Engagement in Literacy Learning

In a student-centered classroom, all students, including those with ADHD, are highly motivated. Students are involved and engaged in learning because they are not being talked at but rather are being asked to think and share their own opinions and perceptions about the learning. The opportunity to share their thinking and

> Students are involved and engaged in learning because they are not being talked at but rather are being asked to think and share their own opinions and perceptions about the learning.

to have their thoughts respected is a much more effective motivator than extrinsic rewards such as grades or even tangible reinforcers.

In addition to active participation in learning, another powerful motivator is allowing students to develop their own goals and work toward them. When students develop their own goals and monitor them carefully by providing explicit feedback, they will work hard and work specifically toward meeting that goal. The fact that students can monitor and see their own progress makes it more likely that they will sustain their efforts until they reach the goal.[16]

Boardman and her colleagues suggest that students' goals should center on content goals, to increase their motivation for reading.[17] Content goals emphasize the importance of learning from what we read and increase students' interest in doing so. Content goals create a purpose for reading because they are grounded in the attainment of conceptual knowledge. When students with ADHD are concentrating and learning about something that interests them, they will read in order to find out more about that interest. In content area classrooms, interest can be created through hands-on activities or other stimulating tasks that pique the students' curiosity and create a reason or need to do research. As content goals are monitored and students realize that they are able to answer the questions that they had or have learned the concepts that they were curious about, the feedback creates a greater incentive to continue to read. Goal setting and feedback on content goals creates a purpose and meaning for reading that will engage and motivate even students who struggle with sustained attention and motivation.

> Creating curiosity about a concept will drive the student to read. Requiring them to read *x* number of pages each night is ineffective.

In addition to feedback and goal setting, a student-centered English language arts class provides a positive learning environment that promotes students' autonomy by allowing them to make choices about topics, forms of communication, and selection of materials, compelling students to assume greater ownership over their own learning. Ensuring that the materials read and the topics covered are more relevant to the students' own life experiences is another factor that contributes positively toward a motivated and engaged student.

Intensive Individualized Interventions

Because 25 to 30 percent of students with ADHD have concomitant learning disabilities,[18] it is essential that schools and districts provide these students with the specific supports they need to be successful with literacy. Not all students with ADHD struggle with reading, but for those who do, it is imperative that supports beyond general classroom instruction be made available. Many students with ADHD do not see themselves as successful students or as very strong readers, and they do not expect to do well in class. In a student-centered classroom, they are often surprised that they are learning and that they are being successful, and they may begin to believe in themselves as students. Despite the positive environment and the scaffolds provided in this type of classroom, some students have struggled so long without support that they may lack some of the skills that are necessary to be considered proficient in grade-level skills. For these students, interventions may be necessary. Interventions do not need to mean that students need to "go to special ed" or to a "resource room" to get "interventions." Although separate instruction is a model that is used in many states for students with significant reading disabilities, for most students, the additional intervention needed to accelerate learning can occur in a general education core classroom that uses differentiated instruction and effective research-based literacy strategies such as those discussed in this chapter and the preceding one. Whichever way the services are delivered, for students who lack fundamental skills because of gaps in learning due to inattention or gaps in learning due to learning disabilities, additional targeted instructional time is needed to fill in these gaps.

> Interventions do not need to mean that students need to "go to special ed" or to a "resource room" to get "interventions."

Many secondary schools today have moved toward using a block schedule that allows students more time in each content area. Some teachers struggle with how to use all this extra time, but the extra time is a gift. Extra time allows the teacher to work with students who need targeted small-group instruction similar to that provided in elementary classrooms. In small groups, the general education teacher, reading specialist, or other specialists or support staff can work with students who need additional instruction on specific skills.

The specific skills that should be part of an intensive intervention are word study and fluency practice.[19] Word study skills allow students to analyze words by meaning and structure. Students are taught to break words into syllable types, to read multisyllabic words by breaking them into parts and then putting them back together, and to recognize which words are irregular and cannot be decoded phonetically. Teaching students to recognize and know the meaning of common prefixes, suffixes, inflectional endings, and root words also increases their ability to attack words in order to determine their meaning.[20]

Fluency and accurate word reading have an effect on reading comprehension. Because of their issues pertaining to working memory, students with ADHD struggle significantly with comprehension when they decode slowly and struggle with word meaning. Developing fluency skills is essential to helping them become more proficient readers. Intervention should provide opportunities for repeated readings of known text and even more opportunities for reading unpracticed passages.[21] Repeated readings allow students to improve their sight vocabulary, which improves fluency. Non-repetitive reading is effective when the text has known words and there is someone to give the student feedback and support while he reads. Fluency is one area that is easily monitored, providing the student with positive feedback that will encourage him to continue to work on developing greater fluency skills.

For schools not on block schedules, some students can receive intensive intervention and extra time to access the core instruction with additional support in a "shadow" class or core "plus" class in which the student has an additional period to receive instruction in word study and fluency and can experience re-teaching and pre-teaching of concepts related to the core curriculum. In this type of English language arts class, students can spend more time on instruction in reading and vocabulary skills, access a text using electronic media, or engage in small-group discussions to help them learn strategies that will help them gain grade-level skills.

Writing Instruction

Because writing demands that students plan, generate content, organize their thoughts, and then translate content into written language, students with ADHD often struggle significantly in this area. Weaknesses in executive functions affect students' ability to use a deliberate, planful, and organized approach to attack the writing task. Specific strategies that address these weaknesses must be part of the instructional process in order to support students with ADHD in becoming successful writers.

Instruction in Self-Regulation Strategies

One effective way to assist students in their writing efforts is by teaching them self-regulation. The self-regulated strategy development (SRSD) model supports students with ADHD who struggle with establishing goals, holding goals in memory, persisting in efforts toward goal completion, and shaping and directing behavior in order to achieve the goal.[22] In the SRSD model, goals are discussed, developed, and very closely monitored. The student's monitoring of the goal is the self-regulation part of the strategy. Deficits in working memory are addressed by breaking the writing task into small parts, teaching specific strategies, and providing prompts, cues, and graphic organizers to support writing efforts in small bits and pieces. This process also has the motivational benefits that were discussed earlier in this chapter in the "Motivation and Engagement in Literacy Learning" section.

Planning Strategies

One example of a specific writing strategy is a three-step planning strategy for writing opinion essays. The planning strategy POW requires students to

1. Plan their essay by choosing a topic.
2. Organize their notes and ideas into a writing plan.
3. Write the essay, using their plan.[23]

While some students will be able to easily take notes and create a writing plan, students with ADHD will need additional scaffolding in this area. The TREE strategy creates a genre-specific framework for a persuasive essay—TREE: Topic sentence, Reason, Explanation, and Ending.[24] For the "T", the topic sentence, the student is guided with the instruction "Tell what you believe, clearly and concisely," reinforcing that the topic sentence makes clear what the author's opinion is. For the "R", the student is told to provide three reasons to support her opinion. Once the student has developed these three reasons, she develops three examples to support each reason (the first "E",). Finally, for the second "E", the student develops an ending. This statement should finish the essay and usually reiterates the opinion. With this kind of specific step-by-step scaffolding, especially when provided within the framework of a graphic organizer, even reluctant writers can organize their writing prior to the "writing" part of the POW strategy. Used together, these two strategies support the student with ADHD by reducing the demands on working memory while they develop their writing.

> **T**-Topic Sentence
> **R**-Reasons
> **E**-Examples
> **E**-Ending

Including this structure alone may be enough to support many students with ADHD, but some may need further reinforcement in order to expand and improve their writing over time. For example, the self-monitoring of the SRSD instruction can be used to help students challenge themselves to write more by simply monitoring word count and the number of TREE essay elements found in their writing. Graphing growth in word count from one draft to another or one writing project to another will push students to try to write more and provide more explicit details and examples in their writing. When students see that they have included more and more TREE essay elements in their writing without reminders, they will begin to use these strategies automatically and improve the overall quality of their essays.

Giving students with ADHD a specific formula for writing provides them with the scaffold they need in order to be successful writers. Similar writing scaffolds and specific writing supports can be found at Easy Essay (*http://www.easyessay.com*), a free site that teaches students how to logically organize an essay or speech about any fact, concept, or idea, providing specific directions and scaffolds for each step.

To Sum Up

English class is usually not the favorite subject of most students with ADHD. This statement can be changed by teachers of English language arts who use a student-centered learning approach to open the door of literacy for these students.

Providing students with exciting opportunities to think, act, react, discuss literature, and use tools and strategies that support organization and development of important skills will help them find that reading can be enjoyable and useful and that writing can be an outlet for the creativity that resides in them. You can make literacy alive for your students, even those with ADHD.

Chapter 5

Strategies to Support Students with ADHD in Math

Teachers of math may wonder why their students with the ADHD label struggle with math. This is a reasonable question. Students with attentional issues would not automatically be considered at risk for math difficulties, but recent research has shown that there is actually a high correlation between ADHD and math difficulties. While on the whole, 4–7 percent of the school-age population experience some form of math difficulty,[1] 26 percent of students with ADHD are found to have a specific math disability.[2]

These students with ADHD have been found to have the weaknesses in working memory that I discussed in earlier chapters, and this is why they struggle with math. Working memory allows a student to manipulate verbal and nonverbal information while he is working to solve math problems, especially in the areas of algorithm knowledge and problem solving.[3] Research by Douglas Fuchs and his colleagues points out that attentional issues—specifically, the inability to block extraneous stimuli from interfering with working memory—are significant.[4]

> Twenty-six percent of students with ADHD are found to have a specific math disability.

Students with ADHD who also have math disability struggle with basic concepts such as number sense and the mastery of basic addition, subtraction, multiplication, and division facts. They struggle with memorizing these facts and cannot retrieve them with the same ease and fluency as their unaffected peers.[5]

Given their attentional issues and issues with working memory, including difficulties in processing the instructional language of math, students with ADHD in your classroom are likely to struggle with daily math instruction.

Mathematical Knowledge

In identifying which strategies support the needs of students who struggle with learning math concepts, it is essential to understand what mathematical abilities are necessary. This understanding will help you recognize in what areas students may need support and how explicit instruction can help them. Students who are successful in math and have a strong "math sense" have developed skills in the following areas:

- Procedural knowledge
- Procedural flexibility
- Conceptual knowledge

Procedural knowledge refers to knowledge of basic skills or the sequence of steps needed to solve a math problem. Procedural knowledge enables a student to execute the necessary action sequences to solve problems.[6] Students with executive function weaknesses struggle significantly in the area of procedural knowledge. Weaknesses in procedural knowledge affect a student's overall ability to be successful in math even when the student has a strong conceptual understanding. Such a student may be able to quickly and adeptly solve long division problems in his head or determine percentages in a circle graph without going through a step-by-step process. When grades depend on students' showing their work, many students with ADHD obtain only failing grades. These students are not able to cognitively organize the process steps in their head even when they are able to grasp the concept.

Procedural flexibility refers to knowing the many different ways in which a particular problem can be solved. Students with strong procedural flexibility realize that a given problem can be solved in a variety of ways, allowing them to solve problems by trying a variety of processes in order to find the solution. This strategy is essential for students with ADHD who struggle with performance inconsistency. On a particular occasion when a student is unable to retrieve one particular process to solve a problem, she can fall back on another process that will get her to the same answer.

Conceptual knowledge is a holistic grasp of the mathematical concept and ideas that are not problem-specific and therefore can be applied to any problem-solving situation. For example, once a student has a clear understanding of fractions, he can use any number of strategies to add, subtract, multiply, and divide fractions without having to rely on one memorized process or algorithm.

The Research

The Center on Instruction recently identified approaches to instruction and curricular design that support the needs of students with learning disabilities and others who struggle with learning math concepts.[7] These instructional strategies include age-old teaching practices that most teachers have employed for some time. While there is nothing new about these practices, the research continues to validate them as effective instructional practices for students with learning disabilities and others at risk, including students with ADHD.

The following practices were found to enhance the mathematical performance of students with learning disabilities and other at-risk learners.[8]

1. Explicit instruction

2. Student verbalization of their mathematical reasoning

3. Visual representations

4. Range and sequence of examples

5. Multiple and heuristic strategies

6. Giving teachers ongoing formative assessment data and feedback on students' mathematics performance

7. Providing data and feedback to students on their mathematical performance

8. Peer-assisted mathematics instruction

From these findings, the Center on Instruction has identified seven instructional practices for teaching mathematics to K–12 students with learning disabilities and other students at risk, including those with ADHD.[9] The instructional recommendations include the following:

1. Teach students by using explicit instruction on a regular basis. Explicit math instruction incorporates step-by-step, problem-specific instruction. This type of instruction should play a key role in mathematics instruction. This practice includes explicit instruction and extensive modeling of each step in the process that is necessary to reach the solution.[10] The teacher provides extra explicit instruction by using think-aloud strategies to show students how competent math problem solvers think through the problem-solving process. Students with ADHD benefit from graphic organizers or guided notes that help them recognize and write down the necessary steps in the thinking processes as they are identified by the teacher during the modeling. This relieves the load on working memory because the steps are written down for later reference. Students then must also be provided with opportunities to use these problem-solving steps so that the teacher can monitor and provide corrective feedback as needed.

> Using think-aloud strategies shows students how competent math problem solvers think through the problem-solving process.

2. Teach students by using multiple instructional examples. Carefully sequenced examples of the problem-solving process for initial learning of new skills are essential for students with ADHD. Because these students struggle with executive functions in the area of sequencing, this strategy, along with the support of graphic organizers or advance organizers, will help them organize a meaningful sequence for problem solving. Once initial learning has been established, it is important that a range of examples continue to be provided so that students can transfer new skills to new situations. Multiple examples can be presented in a specific sequence or pattern such as concrete to abstract, easy to hard, or simple to complex. For example, fractions and algebraic equations can be taught first with concrete examples, then with pictorial representations, and finally in an abstract manner.[11] Students can be taught to recognize critical features of problems—for example, clue words are excellent markers that help students make decisions about various strategies they can use to solve a problem. It may be helpful to make a chart of some math clue words:

Addition	Subtraction
Sum	Difference
Total	How much more
In all	Exceed
Perimeter	Left

Multiplication	Division
Product	Share
Total	Distribute
Area	Quotient
Times	Average

3. Have students verbalize decisions and solutions to a math problem. Encouraging students to verbalize or think aloud about their decisions and solutions to math problems is an essential aspect of scaffolded instruction.[12]

This practice involves having students verbalize the steps in a solution format—for example, "First add the numbers in the units column. Write down the answer. Then add the numbers in the tens column . . ."[13] Verbalization of mathematical reasoning can also include a self-questioning format in which the student goes through a series of questions and answers that allows him to walk through the problem-solving process. These strategies have great potential for students with ADHD, who often struggle with internal language and impulsivity.[14] Students with ADHD and other learning disabilities frequently attempt to solve multi-step problems by randomly combining numbers rather than implementing step-by-step solutions or any problem-solving strategy. Because these students often don't use internal language to regulate their thinking, verbalization may help them to order their thinking during problem solving.

> Encouraging students to verbalize or think aloud about their decisions and solutions to math problems is an essential aspect of scaffolded instruction.

4. Teach students to visually represent the information in a math problem. Visually representing math problems has long been known as a helpful strategy that supports the learning of mathematical concepts for all students. The use of graphics and diagrams as visual representations of math concepts has a proven track record of improving students' conceptual understanding of math processes. Teacher-directed visual representations used as a part of a multi-step approach to instruction have had the most success. This process, directed by the teacher, helps the student to first identify what type of problem she has been given and then create a corresponding diagram that represents the essential information and the mathematical procedure necessary to find the unknown. Then the student translates the diagram into a math sentence and solves it.[15] This process is extremely beneficial for students with ADHD; again, the diagram frees up working memory because the basic information is stored visually in the diagram and the student is able to refer back to it in order to create the math sentence.

5. Teach students to solve problems using multiple or heuristic strategies. Multiple and heuristic strategy instruction appears to be an important supplement to explicit instruction. These strategies provide a generic problem-solving guide in which the strategies or specific steps are not problem-specific. For example, a heuristic strategy can include steps such as "Read the problem. Highlight the key words. Solve the problems. Check your work."[16] Heuristics can be used in organizing information and solving a range of math problems. They usually include

> Students are exposed to multiple strategies and then are encouraged to use an appropriate strategy from a menu of options rather than one problem-specific process that relies heavily on memorization.

student discourse and reflection on evaluating alternative solutions. In this process, students are exposed to multiple strategies and then are encouraged to use an appropriate strategy from a menu of options rather than one problem-specific process that relies heavily on memorization. Students with ADHD benefit from this strategy because it supports the organization of information and reflection on the efficiency of choices made in the problem-solving process.

6. Provide ongoing formative assessment data and feedback to teachers. When teachers perform ongoing formative assessment and evaluation of student progress in math, they are able to identify students who have not yet grasped a concept and are able to adjust their instruction in order to support these students. In addition, when teachers are provided with specific strategies and instructional tips on what to teach, when to introduce a new skill, and how to group students based on performance data, student performance increases.[17] When teachers regularly reflect on what skills their students have improved on in the past two weeks and what they can do to improve student performance on targeted skills, instruction and student outcomes improve.[18]

7. Provide peer-assisted instruction to students. The approach of students teaching other students allows students to learn from each other as they each play both the role of the tutor or teacher and the role of the tutee or student. The more traditional type of cross-age peer tutoring, in which a student of a higher grade level provides tutoring to a younger student, has proven effective but is not always viable in a secondary school classroom. Strategically pairing a higher-performing student and a student with ADHD who is struggling is often effective. Allowing the student with ADHD to verbalize learning while tutoring her partner is another way to implement the verbalization strategy.

The Practice

Research has identified the instructional practices in the preceding section as effective in meeting the needs of students with mathematical learning disabilities or students at risk for math problems. How can this research be put into practice in your classroom? The strategies presented in this section will provide you with specific tools to bring the research into effective practice with your students in your classroom.

Math Problem-Solving Strategies

When students with ADHD have not acquired the skills to know what to do when they are confronted with word problems in their secondary school textbooks or in real-world math problems, they are unable to disaggregate the necessary information in order to systematically move toward a solution. There are many reasons for the paralysis they may experience when faced with these types of problems.

Mathematical problem solving is a complex cognitive activity that involves a number of processes and strategies. Problem solving has two stages: problem representation and problem execution. Successful problem solving is not possible without first being able to represent the problem appropriately. Appropriate problem representation is essential to understanding the problem and being able to develop a plan or steps to solve it. Students who struggle with representing math problems will have significant problems in solving them. Students with ADHD who struggle with executive functions in the area of activation struggle with the processes of organization, prioritization, and activating to begin work. This is the point where the student is not able to sort out where to begin to solve the problem or to identify the critical details necessary to determine the first step. Few students recognize the need to acquire problem representational strategies as a necessary first step in the problem-solving process.

Visualization

Visualization is a very powerful representation strategy, but most students do not develop this strategy automatically because this is not a regular practice for students whose teachers have relied heavily on textbooks to guide instruction. Textbooks may instruct students to draw a picture, but many students draw a picture without considering the relationship among the problem components and as a result still do not understand how to solve the problem.[19] Rather than just drawing the problem, it is drawing the problem correctly that will allow the

> Immature pictorial representations do not support the student in reaching a solution.

student to use the visualization as a tool to develop a plan. Effective schematic visualization shows a relationship among the problem parts.[20] According to Marjorie Montague, poor problem solvers make immature representations that are more pictorial than schematic in nature (see Figure 5.1).

Other cognitive processes needed for effective problem solving include

- Reading the problem for understanding
- Paraphrasing the problem by putting it into one's own words
- Hypothesizing or making a plan to solve the problem
- Estimating or predicting the outcome
- Computing or doing the arithmetic
- Checking to make sure the plan was appropriate and the answer is correct[21]

Mr. Swanson needs 12 gallons of brown paint at $9.95 a gallon. He needs to buy three brushes at $2.45 each. How much does he spend in total?

Pictorial   Schematic

Figure 5.1: Pictorial Versus Schematic Representations
of a Math Problem

Students who are poor mathematical problem solvers do not process problem information efficiently or effectively. Due to executive function weaknesses, they lack the self-regulation strategies and the metacognitive processes to understand, analyze, solve, and evaluate the problem. Teachers must understand and directly teach these processes to students so that they can develop problem-solving skills.

Process Steps

Using process steps ensures that students use self-regulation strategies such as telling themselves what to do, asking questions, and evaluating and monitoring outcomes. Students with ADHD who struggle with executive functions in complex problem solving will certainly struggle with this problem-solving process unless scaffolding, direct instruction, and practice with the process are provided. They need to be taught specifically what good problem solvers do through explicit strategy instruction.

Marjorie Montague recommends using an acronym to help students remember the problem-solving steps. These steps must be taught directly, and this process is one of the heuristic strategies discussed in the Center on Instruction research. The acronym RPV-HECC was created for math problem solving. The acronym stands for the following problem-solving process steps described by Montague:[22]

R = Read for understanding

Say: Read the problem. If I don't understand, read it again.

Ask: Have I read and understood the problem?

Check: For understanding as I solve the problem.

P = Paraphrase in your own words

Say: Underline the important information. Put the problem in my own words.

Ask: Have I underlined the important information? What is the question? What am I looking for?

Check: That the information goes with the question.

V = Visualize a picture or diagram

Say: Make a drawing or a diagram. Show the relationships among the problem parts.

Ask: Does the picture fit the problem? Did I show the relationships?

Check: The picture against the problem information.

H = Hypothesize a plan to solve the problem

Say: Decide how many steps and operations are needed. Write the operations symbols ($=, -, \times, /$).

Ask: If I . . . , what will I get? If I . . . , then what do I need to do next? How many steps are needed?

Check: That the plan makes sense.

E = Estimate or predict an answer

Say: Round the numbers, do the problem in my head, and write the estimate.

Ask: Did I round up or down? Did I write the estimate?

Check: That I used the important information.

C = Compute or do the arithmetic

Say: Do the operations in the right order.

Ask: How does my answer compare with my estimate? Does my answer make sense? Are the decimals or money signs in the right place?

Check: That all operations were done in the right order.

C = Check or make sure everything is right

Say: Check the plan to make sure it is right. Check the computation.

Ask: Have I checked every step? Have I checked the computation? Is my answer right?

Check: That everything is right. If not, go back. Ask for help if I need it.

In order for students to learn to effectively use this problem-solving strategy, they must practice it, verbally rehearsing it until they can recite it from memory, using the acronym as a scaffold for all the processes. The teacher will also need to model the process, thinking aloud about his strategies as he solves problems, modeling for students the effective and efficient use of the strategies. The teacher should also allow students to play the role of the teacher, modeling the use of the strategies for the class. Teachers will also need to model for students how to construct a picture that effectively demonstrates the relationships among the parts of the problem. Creating this picture allows students to learn how to select the important information to correctly develop a schematic representation of the problem. As students become more familiar with the process, the teacher should provide more opportunities for students to play the role of the teacher in front of the class and with partners in a peer coaching model.

Mnemonic Instructional Strategies

Mnemonic instruction is a set of strategies designed to help students improve their memory for new information. Mnemonic instruction links new information to previous knowledge through the use of visual or acoustic cues.

There are three basic types of mnemonic strategies:

- **Keyword:** A familiar word that sounds similar to the word or idea being taught. Keywords are generally used with some sort of illustration to help the student make connections between the old and the new information.

- **Pegword:** A set of rhyming words that are used to represent numbers. For example, the pegword for one is *bun*. Pegwords are used to help students remember information involving numbers or other information in a particular order. Rhyming words help them associate the number with the word. For example, the pegword for six is *sticks*. The student draws sticks to represent the number six. The student then solves, using the pegwords: Bun (1) times Sticks (6) would be 1 × 6, equaling Sticks (6). Sticks (6) times Sticks (6) equals Dirty Sticks (36). The visual representation helps students learn the concepts along with the pegwords.[23]

- **Acronyms:** Expressions formed from the first letter of a sequence of words. Acronyms are used to help students remember information—for example, the RPV-HECC acronym described earlier in this chapter is used by students to help them remember the steps of the problem-solving process. Acronyms are also used in math to teach math facts, the order of operations, measurement, and geometry as well as problem solving. Sentences such as "Please Excuse My Dear Aunt Sally," which is commonly used to teach students the order of operations (parenthesis, exponents, multiply, divide, add, subtract), are another effective memory device.

All three types of mnemonics are used to teach math. The pegword strategy is geared exclusively for math because it is designed specifically to help students remember numeric information, especially in a particular sequence. Again, it is essential that the teacher take the time to explicitly teach these strategies. Teachers have to show students how they can create mnemonics themselves, how to practice using a mnemonic, and give students ample time to practice all aspects of the strategy until they can use it independently to retrieve the correct information.

Concrete-Representational-Abstract Instructional Strategy

In the three-part concrete-representational-abstract (CRA) instructional strategy, each part builds on the previous part to promote student learning and retention so that the student can gain greater conceptual knowledge.[24] The CRA instructional sequence consists of three stages:

- **Concrete:** The teacher models instruction with concrete materials. The use of manipulatives is commonly part of this stage.

- **Representational:** The teacher transforms the concrete model to a semi-concrete model, which typically includes drawings or some other visual representation.

- **Abstract:** The teacher models math concepts at the symbolic level, using only numbers, notation, and mathematical symbols to represent the numeric concept.

The CRA approach supports the needs of students with ADHD by creating a sequence or process for organizing information. It allows students to actually learn the underlying concepts rather than simply memorizing a rule that must be applied in certain situations. Taking the information and making it visual in the representational state also helps free up the student's working memory so that it can be more effectively used for the abstract thinking necessary to solve the problem.

The CRA sequence of instruction provides a graduated, scaffolded approach that helps students to create meaningful connections among the concrete, or the "doing" stage; the representational, the "seeing" stage; and the abstract, or symbolic stage of math understanding. In terms of learning modalities, the CRA sequence uses visual and tactile or kinesthetic experiences to establish mathematical understanding.

Graphic Organizer Strategies

Students with ADHD who struggle with working memory and executive functions find it hard to identify key information, discard nonessential information, make connections between broad concepts and details, sustain focus, persist through multi-step problems, or use any specific strategic approach to solve problems. These students struggle with complex, open-ended problems that require them to identify and use only relevant information and systematically determine how to solve the problem using the correct symbolic representation and operation. If students have been taught to use the problem-solving, mnemonics, and CRA strategies mentioned earlier in this section, they may have found some way to strategically approach problems, especially word problems.[25]

The strategies that were discussed earlier in this chapter use verbal and visual processes to retrieve information, but do not focus on how students should organize the information so that the salient information is highlighted and stored for manipulation and use in the abstract stage. Graphic organizers are diagrammatic illustrations that are used to organize and highlight key content information or vocabulary.[26] Graphic organizers allow the student to maintain the information over time, creating a greater chance of moving the information into long-term memory.

Common graphic organizers used in math instruction include hierarchical diagrams, sequence charts, and compare-and-contrast charts.[27]

Hierarchical diagrams have a main branch for the overall concept or information, followed by connected subsidiary branches linked by arrows, lines, colors, numbers, or phrases that show the connections. The example in Figure 5.2 shows a hierarchical graphic display that has polynomials as its main branch and monomials, binomials, and trinomials as subsidiary branches, in different fonts to aid memory and recall.

Sequence charts represent a sequence of events or procedures in a particular content area (see Figure 5.3). Arrows and numbers are usually used to make the sequence clear.

Polynomials		
Monomial (polynomial of one term)	Binomial (polynomial of two terms)	*Trinomial (polynomial of three terms)*
5	5a + 5b	*5a + 6c + 12d*
X	10h + 10i	*x + 2x^2 + 4x^3*
5b	10 + 12d	*4x^2 + 3x^2 + 6x* (non-example)
1/5	7y – 2x	*3 + 4x + x^2*
10/2	3x – 4x (non-example)	
5a + 5a		

Figure 5.2: Hierarchical Graphic Organizer

Polya's
Four Problem-Solving Steps

1. Understand the Problem (What is the goal? Draw a representation.)

2. Devise a Plan (Is there a similar problem I can relate to this?)

3. Carry Out the Plan (Carry out the plan, and check each step.)

4. Look Back (Check answer.)

Figure 5.3: Sequence Chart

Compare-and-contrast charts highlight differences and similarities across two or three ideas or sets of information. A common effective strategy for comparison and contrast that was identified by Robert Marzano, Debra Pickering, and Jane Pollock in 2001 is the use of a Venn diagram (see Figure 5.4).[28]

Consistent use of graphic organizers (see Figure 5.5) will help students with ADHD to sequence and organize information as well as grasp related concepts, supporting them in obtaining the procedural knowledge and conceptual knowledge needed to solve math problems. To help students create effective graphic organizers, it is important for the teacher to model or provide models as a scaffold in the development of this instructional strategy. Initially, teachers may need to provide the graphic organizer itself with some of the information filled in, but eventually this type of scaffold will be faded as students learn to recognize where information might go on a particular type of graphic organizer.

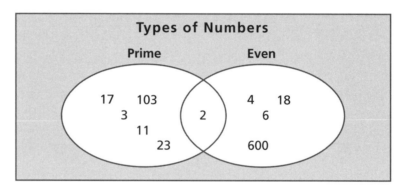

Figure 5.4: Compare-and-Contrast Chart, or Venn Diagram

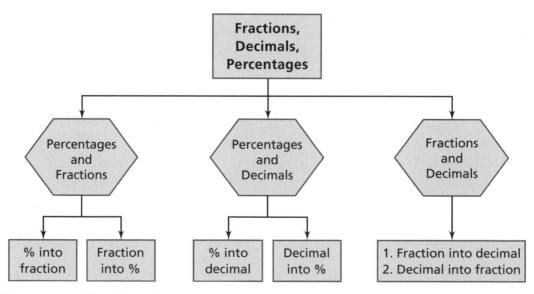

Figure 5.5: Graphic Organizer on Fractions, Decimals, and Percentages

Strategies for Teaching Adolescents with ADHD

As students acquire practice with numerous types of graphic organizers, they will recognize which organizers are more appropriate for a particular problem-solving process.

Putting It All Together: Strategies for Accessing Algebraic Concepts

So far, we have discussed the instructional strategies identified through the Center on Instruction and have applied those in several practical classroom strategies that will support students with ADHD and other mathematical learning problems. Currently, there is much controversy over the importance of algebra as a gateway skill to higher levels of math and to general success in our society. In the past, students with learning problems were not given the opportunity to learn algebra and were often offered "consumer math" classes instead. Although this controversy still rages across states today, the Access Center has identified strategies that support access to algebraic concepts for all students.[29] Many of the strategies that have already been discussed in this chapter are also found to be effective tools for teaching students algebraic skills.

Many students with math difficulties, including those with ADHD, face the following challenges when it comes to moving beyond basic math to algebra.

- Translating word problems into mathematical symbols
- Distinguishing patterns from detail information
- Describing or paraphrasing an explanation
- Linking the concrete to a representation and then to an abstract concept
- Remembering vocabulary and processes
- Showing fluency with basic number operations
- Maintaining focus for a period of time
- Showing written work

To help students overcome these challenges, it is essential that instructional and learning strategies address the issues that students with ADHD face due to problems with memory, communication and language, processing, attention, organizational skills, and math anxiety. Instructional and learning methods that can be used to deliver a variety of content objectives and that facilitate the integration, manipulation, storage, and retrieval of information include

- Mnemonics
- Concrete-representational-abstract (CRA) instruction
- Graphic organizers

Mnemonics Example in Algebra

Mnemonics help students with ADHD to improve their memory for new information, allowing them to link information to prior knowledge through both visual and auditory cues. The DRAW mnemonic provides a scaffold that helps students remember the process steps for solving an algebraic equation. This strategy includes the following steps:

- Discover the variable.

- Read the equation, identify the operations, and think about the process for solving the equation.

- Answer the equation.

- Write the answer and check the equation.

For example, in Figure 5.6, the student takes the equation $4x + 2x = 12$ and initially *discovers* the variable. She represents the variable x with the circles. Then, she *reads* the equation and identifies the operation of addition, whereby she combines like terms, determining that there are six x's. She thinks about the process for solving the equation $6x = 12$, which would be to divide the total of 12 equally among the six circles. The number of tallies represented in one circle would represent the value of the variable x. Using this process, she finds the *answer* to the equation. She then *writes* that answer to the equation: $x = 2$. Finally, she checks the equation to make sure her answer was correct: $4(2) + 2(2) = 8 + 4 = 12$.

Concrete-Representational-Abstract Example in Algebra

Using the CRA method, initally, students use manipulatives to determine how they might balance an equation. The picture of the equation reminds students that

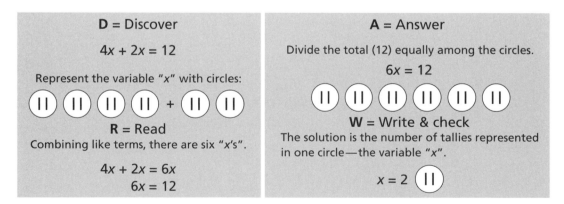

Figure 5.6: Problem Solving using the DRAW Mnemonic

Strategies for Teaching Adolescents with ADHD

both sides must be equal to, or balance to the same number (Figure 5.7a). Then, they are given manipulatives or concrete objects to find out how many squares and triangles are needed to balance the equation. The students are reminded that the triangle represents the same number on both sides of the equation and that each square represents the same number. The next step is to move to the representation stage, where they write the equation, using pictures of the manipulatives to represent the variables (Figure 5.7b). Using the manipulatives, the students then determine the solution as seen in the top part of Figure 5.7c. They then take that representation to the abstract stage, using number symbols to represent the solution to the equation, as shown in the bottom part of Figure 5.7c.

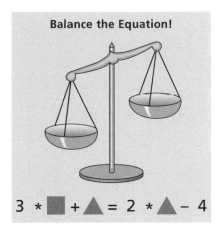

Figure 5.7a: Picture of an Equation for Use as a Starting Point in Concrete Representation of an Equation Through Manipulatives

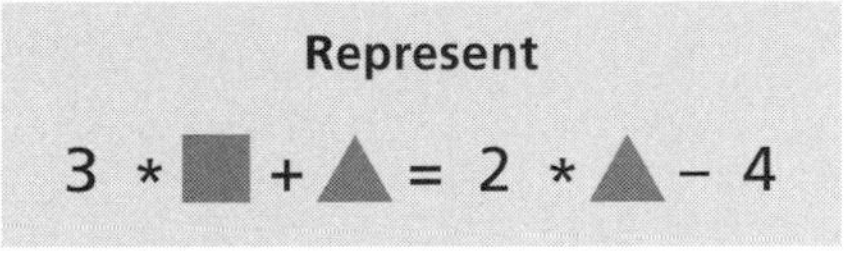

Represent

$$3 * \blacksquare + \blacktriangle = 2 * \blacktriangle - 4$$

Figure 5.7b: Semi-Concrete Representation of an Equation

Solution

$$3 * \blacksquare + \blacktriangle = 2 * \blacktriangle - 4$$

$$3 * 1 + 7 = 2 * 7 - 4$$

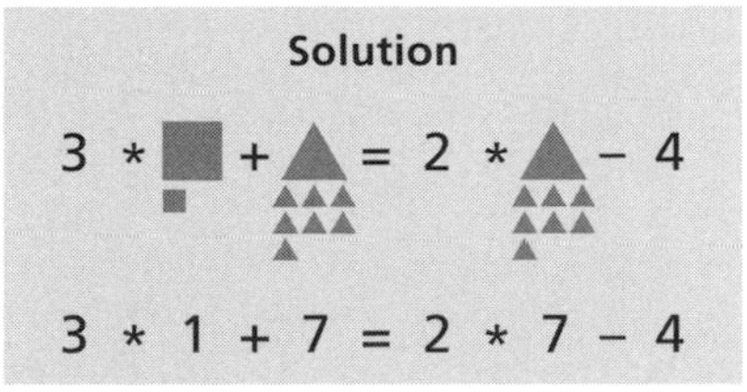

Figure 5.7c: Solution and Abstract Representation of an Equation

Graphic Organizer Examples in Algebra

Graphic organizers are tools that connect content in a meaningful way to help students organize and maintain information over time. They are the most effective when they are used consistently and are integrated into the instruction through creative approaches.[30] Effective graphic organizers for algebra instruction include hierarchical diagramming (Figure 5.8), sequence charts, and compare-and-contrast charts (Figure 5.9).

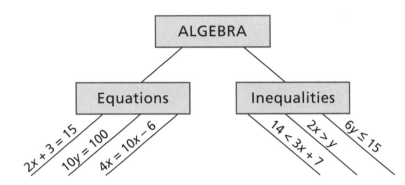

Figure 5.8: Example of a Hierarchical Graphic Organizer

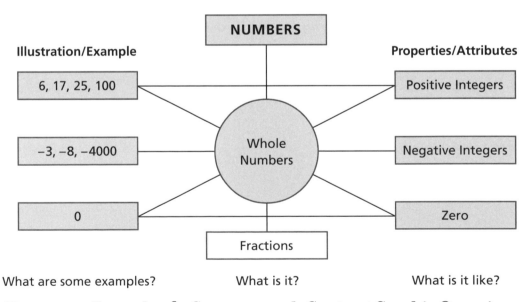

Figure 5.9: Example of a Compare-and-Contrast Graphic Organizer

To Sum Up

Since 26 percent of all students with ADHD have a specific math disability,[31] it is essential that math teachers employ research-based instructional strategies that meet the specific needs of these students. Your students with ADHD and a concomitant math disability can learn the math skills that you are responsible for teaching; however, ongoing difficulties with executive functions, limited working memory, and attentional issues make it difficult for them to be successful. Implementation and consistent use of research-based instructional strategies in your math classroom will allow your students with ADHD to meet content standards and pass state assessments, learn to master basic skills and algebraic concepts, and learn the lifelong problem-solving skills needed for ongoing success in mathematics.

Chapter 6

Strategies to Support Students with ADHD in Science and Social Studies

In the preceding chapters, you have discovered numerous research-based teaching strategies that can easily be applied to any content area. The strategies and lesson design discussed in this chapter will provide you with examples of how these strategies can be employed in science and social science classrooms.

As you may recall from Chapter Four, when teachers nurture a learner-centered classroom rather than a content-centered classroom, all students have a greater opportunity to learn and students with ADHD find themselves more engaged in the learning. In a learner-centered classroom, acquisition of the content in meaningful ways is the focus. The strategies discussed in this chapter will focus on helping students with ADHD grasp the concepts and, through strategy instruction, provide them ways to use this content knowledge in both classroom applications and the real world.

> In a learner-centered classroom, acquisition of the content in meaningful ways is the focus.

The reason that students with ADHD often complain about their science and social studies classes is not that the content is boring but rather that the learning is not active enough to keep their attention. They allow their mind to wander off, and so they miss the exciting learning opportunities presented in these subject areas. The key to making science and social studies instruction engaging to students with ADHD is ensuring that the learning that takes place in the classroom is active learning. Given that standards define what is taught but not how it is taught, teachers can delve into their creativity and challenge themselves to making science and history come alive.

The Research: Science

There has been much debate over what constitutes good science instruction. The traditional models of lecture and reading coupled with problem practice, worksheets, and lab activities that prove a learned concept have often been replaced with the reform practices of students working together in small groups, engaging in hands-on activities, and focusing on topics based on student preference.[1] Research has shown that it is not an either-or choice; good science instruction needs to include the traditional lecture and reading as well as hands-on lab activities.[2] Students can be engaged during a dynamic lecture, or they can sit passively through a boring one that does not hold their attention and has no meaning for them. Conversely, lab experiments alone are not the epitome of good science instruction if they are done simply as an activity for activity's sake and are not related to a learning goal. Good instruction provides a balance of hands-on instruction that motivates students and allows them to collect and think about data as well as lecture and reading that supports them in making sense of the data.

Research points to five main elements of instruction that are critical to student learning:

- Motivation
- Elicitation of prior knowledge
- Intellectual engagement
- Use of evidence
- Sense making[3]

Motivation is created by instruction that hooks students by addressing something they have wondered about or can be induced to wonder about. An active learning strategy connected to an anticipation guide can often create this opportunity for induced wonder and will be discussed further later in this chapter. Eliciting prior knowledge is essential to cognitive change. Students need an opportunity to think about what they currently know or understand about a concept. Strategies that elicit prior knowledge encourage students to recognize their own ideas, confront their ideas, and formulate new ones based on evidence.[4]

Intellectual engagement is more than just student engagement. Science lab activities are usually engaging to students, but too often their purpose has been to allow students to fill out a worksheet to file in the "finished work" box. Intellectual engagement includes meaningful experiences that engage students with important science content while they do the intellectual work of making connections and collecting data for a purpose rather than collecting data in order to practice proper technique.

In order for students to become scientifically literate, they need to be encouraged to view science as a process by which knowledge is constructed, not as a collection of facts. An integral part of this process is the collection and interpretation of data, which are used to determine whether scientific concepts are supported by evidence. Drawing conclusions from evidence is how scientific knowledge is generated, tested, and revised.[5]

> In order for students to become scientifically literate, they need to be encouraged to view science as a process by which knowledge is constructed, not as a collection of facts.

Students also need an opportunity to make connections between what they did in a lesson and what they were intended to learn. Such connections can be accomplished through summarizing what was done and what it means or through comparing prior knowledge and new learning, using a compare-and-contrast format. This process helps students make sense of what they have learned and links prior knowledge to the new learned experience, which is the goal of scientific literacy.

The Practice: Science

Developing scientific curiosity is the key to motivating reluctant learners in science. Developing and nurturing this curiosity is foundational for effective intellectual engagement of all learners, including those with ADHD. In meeting the challenge of finding evidence that supports their suppositions, you can be guaranteed that learning in your science classroom will occur. When a student with ADHD is actively engaged intellectually, is cognitively challenged, and is keenly involved in scientific intellectual heavy lifting, the daily challenge of motivating the unmotivated will disappear.

Motivating Reluctant Learners

There are multiple ways to incorporate research-based critical elements into science instruction. Motivating students to actively participate in science instruction is a challenge, but they can be affected by both extrinsic and intrinsic motivators. Extrinsic motivators such as deadlines, tests, and quizzes are motivating to some students, but rarely work as motivators for students with ADHD. For students who have difficulties with executive functions in the areas of organizing and prioritizing work, deadlines do not motivate them to get it done. In addition, tests and quizzes and their long-term consequences do not matter much when students struggle with focus and regulating effort. Intrinsic motivators such as finding answers to questions stemming from students' own desire to learn are much more effective because they are fueled by students' intellectual curiosity, stimulating students to interact with real-world phenomena through hands-on experiments, computer simulation, teacher-led discussion, or action research on a topic of interest. Students with ADHD will continue to need support to help them with organization and prioritization, but focus, attention, and effort will be less of an issue when students are intellectually engaged in the process.

Eliciting Prior Knowledge

As students move forward into an intellectually engaging project or lesson, eliciting prior knowledge is essential in order for students to understand where they are and what they want to know when they are done with the current study or lesson. K-W-L charts or other demonstrations of current knowledge provide a basis for the research or learning that the student is embarking upon. Posing queries to get students engaged—for example, stating, "All cells are permeable" and having students respond "true" or "false"—is one strategy for assessing prior knowledge and hooking students on the learning process. Accepting incorrect responses allows students to recognize learning later when their incorrect responses are confronted with evidence. This process fosters cognitive change and is much more powerful in helping students with ADHD retain content in long-term memory than simply telling them the right answer.

Intellectual Engagement + Use of Evidence = Making Sense of Science

When a student is given a chance to prove her response to a statement, that student is intellectually engaged. The process for obtaining the needed evidence can be a hands-on activity or other research that may provide the evidence the student needs to prove the statement. This process requires that the student do the intellectual work rather than the teacher; when teachers do all the intellectual heavy lifting, student learning is short-circuited.[6] The student supports her claims through the use of evidence and data. The teacher does need to guide how the evidence is obtained and provide the student with avenues to finding the necessary data, but again, the student is doing the intellectual work. When a student with ADHD is actively engaged intellectually, she will have less difficulty with focusing and sustaining attention and will find science instruction motivating and purposeful.

The Research: Social Studies

There is not much recent research on teaching and learning of instructional strategies for history or social science; however, information literacy skills are very

Strategies for Teaching Adolescents with ADHD

closely related to the intellectual processes that teachers have identified as the "domains of history-social science thinking."[7] Because learners of history and social science obtain all their content through literacy and research, it is essential that students of history and social science be able to appropriately access, evaluate, and use information from a variety of sources.

Given this context, instructional strategies need to focus on helping students put data in their own words, create a logical interpretation of data derived from numerous sources, as well as put this information into a context that allows them to relate to it in a meaningful way. Creating a meaningful context for history and social science concepts is discussed later in this chapter. Without active learning, applying these data is very difficult for the student with ADHD.

Strategies that support students in relating to historical events, people, and eras are essential in creating a meaningful context. During instruction, teachers can employ strategies of comparing and contrasting in which they relate the past to the present, helping students to identify similarities and differences and draw logical conclusions about the social, political, and economic concepts of the time. When students are able to take multiple perspectives or are able to examine a role or position from another point of view, they are more likely to be able to identify and analyze cause and effect in history, as well as obtain a clearer understanding of how multiple influences play a role in history and government.

The Practice: Social Studies

Teachers of history and the social sciences, like science teachers, have the difficult task of making connections between classroom content and their students' lives. How does a history or social science teacher bring the past to life and make these all important connections? The history teacher must make learning an active process that creates meaningful cognitive connections to current events and students' contemporary lives. Once a teacher has made these important connections, all students in her social studies classes, including those with ADHD, will find the study of history or social science a meaningful process that prepares them to be contributing members of society.

Making Connections with History Facts

Facilitating active learning in a social studies classroom consists of ensuring that the instruction appeals to the senses, makes meaningful cognitive connections, and is supported by differentiated instructional practices and specific strategy instruction.

In the article "Facing High Stakes in High School: 25 Successful Strategies from an Inclusive Social Studies Classroom," David Connor and Christopher Lagares share several strategies that support the specific needs of students who struggle with memory, organization, and time management issues common in students with ADHD.[8] They recommend the use of stories, visualization, and repetition to support memorization of major concepts and details in history. An example from the article depicts how Chris teaches his students the amendments to the Constitution:

> This Sunday I visited a big wooden **church** (religion), with a priest reading ***The New York Times*** (press). He then **spoke** (speech) to his **congregation** (assembly) and asked them to sign a **petition** (right to petition). *Now, repeat to me what happened last Sunday . . .*

Students are supported as they repeat this process numerous times, adding more information to each retelling, by having a graphic organizer or advance organizer to help them organize the amendments in order.

Students can also aid memory by creating visual symbols to help them remember key concepts. In Chris's class, some of the students used the following visual symbols to support their long-term memory of the Bill of Rights.[9]

- A human head with an open mouth: free speech

- A gun: right to bear arms

- A house: government may not require people to house soldiers

In addition to difficulties with memorizing key concepts, many students struggle with answering "document-based questions" or DBQs, which ask students to base their responses on a specific document or primary source of information. Many students, including those with ADHD, draw a blank when faced with such questions.[10] Students do not find any connections to these documents and cannot find a way to relate to them. Kylene Beers suggests that students use the following symbols while they read the documents, in order to create as many connections as possible.[11]

S	**Surprising:**	What surprised you in the text?
*	**Important:**	What is important in the text?
?	**Clarification:**	What are you unsure about in the text?
T-T	**Text-to-text connections:**	How does this reading relate to other texts you have read?
T-C	**Text-to-class connections:**	How does this text relate to another lesson in this class?
T-S	**Text-to-self connections:**	How does the text relate to you personally?

Students write these symbols either in the margin or on sticky notes, to create entry points into the text. Using this process provides students with ADHD with a process or sequence for attacking the document in order to gain meaning from the text.

Creating applicable meaning from historical events is the challenge of all history and social science teachers. Using current events is one method of connecting past history with present practices and related issues.[12] Using visuals, role play, or creative content-specific games to enhance and extend learning is another way to bring history to life. The History Alive curriculum allows students to view, touch, and interpret images as well as use movement and introspection to help them to better grasp a moment or feeling that is central to understanding a particular historical event or process.[13] Christopher Lagares designed a similar game to teach his students about the diversity of immigrants in this country (see Table 6.1). This game allows students to use facts and their imagination to create a unique character and obtain a clearer understanding of a particular historical period.[14]

Using Images

Using images is an effective means of constructing meaning from the past and thus is a valuable tool for social studies teachers to use to engage students in active learning. There are numerous ways to use images in classroom instruction. The authors of *Engagement in Teaching History: Theory and Practice for Middle and Secondary Teachers* suggest using three techniques to increase student engagement and create greater meaning for students who are learning history.[15] They suggest that teachers use a think-pair-share strategy along with the images to facilitate discussion.

The first technique is using an image in conjunction with questions pertaining to the people, place, and time in history. The teacher guides the discussion by providing an image on the overhead or screen and then asks students to answer a series of questions related to the person, their place, and their time in history. Students discuss their responses to the questions with a partner and prepare to share them with the class.

The second technique focuses on analyzing an image in order to identify similarities and differences. In this case, two images are displayed and students are directed to identify three similarities between the pictures and three differences between the pictures. Again, students share with a partner or group and identify commonalities in their observations.

The third strategy is using quadrantal or hemispheric analysis of the image. In this strategy, the teacher prepares the students to be careful observers of the image. Initially, they are given a short time (twenty seconds) to observe the image. Once the image is covered up again, the students write down anything they remember. Then the teacher reveals only a quadrant or hemisphere of the picture for the students to view for about thirty seconds, during which they write down everything that they see. This process is repeated until the entire picture has been observed. Once students have shared the details of their observations with their partner or group, they answer guiding questions related to time, place, and historical themes.

Table 6.1: Immigrant Game

Name _____   Period _____

Step 1: Country of Origin	Step 2: Marital Status	Step 3: Children	Step 4: Age	Step 5: Relatives	Step 6: New home town	Step 7: Synthesize
Roll the dice and add up the values to determine what nationality your immigrant character will be:	Roll one die to determine whether you are married, single, or widowed.	Roll one die to determine how many children you have.	Roll the dice to determine your age at the time of immigration.	Roll the dice and add up the values to determine whether you have family in the United States and who that person is. This will determine where you live.	Pick your new home town based on where your relatives or friend might live. If you have no relatives or friends, choose a new home town.	Write a biography or journal entry of your immigrant character on a separate sheet of paper, using details from the game.
	• Even number = married	The value of the die is the number of children that you have with you.	One die is the number in the "tens" place (cannot be 1).	2. Chicago - uncle		Also include:
	• 1 or 3 = widowed		One die is the number in the "ones" place.	3. Milwaukee - brother		• Why did you want to live in America?
Country **Religion**	• 5 = single		For example:	4. Brooklyn - brother		• How did you feel about leaving your home?
2. Dominican Republic — Roman Catholic			First roll = 3	5. Queens - aunt		• What did you expect America to be like?
3. China — Buddhist			Second roll = 6	6. Long Island - aunt		
4. Poland — Jewish			Age = 36	7. Buffalo - sister		• What surprises did you find in America?
5. Hungary — Jewish				8. Atlantic City - sister		• How were you treated by the Americans?
6. Germany — Protestant				9. Bronx - parents		• Add any additional details.
7. Italy — Roman Catholic				10. New York - parents		
8. Ireland — Roman Catholic				11. Newark, NJ - friend		
9. Russia — Jewish				12. No relatives or friends		
10. Lithuania — Jewish						
11. Japan — Buddhist						
12. Spain — Roman Catholic						
Write down your country of origin and your religion.	Write down your marital status.	Write down the number of children that you have.	Write down your age.	Write down where your relatives live.	Write down the name of your new home town.	Write the biography or journal entry. This should be creative and written in paragraph form.

Source: Copyright © 2007 by Christopher Lagares. Adapted and used with permission.

Active Learning in the Science or Social Studies Classroom

In *Instruction for All Students*, Paula Rutherford suggests that when teachers are making decisions about how to optimally engage students, they use the following list to assess their lesson design.[16]

- Students are encouraged to express varied opinions, as long as they support the opinion with data.

- Students are encouraged to think about how the information they are learning relates to other subjects and their lives beyond the school day.

- Students are able to think critically and creatively in response to questions that have more than one answer.

- Students are encouraged to think and discuss answers with a partner or in a small group before answering in the large group.

- Students are encouraged to reflect on their own experiences with learning something new and delve into new ideas or suppositions before lectures or reading.

- Students are supported in examining their own thinking and building on their own ideas.

- Students are informally assessed for prior knowledge on the content before a new unit of instruction is begun.

- Students are made aware of essential questions and key concepts to help them organize new information in a systematic manner.

- Students share the responsibility for generating their own vocabulary lists and the questions that they want answered.

- Students resolve their differences by discussing their thinking.

- Students have the opportunity to practice skills and facts during class time so that they can use them independently in the future.

- Students are encouraged to try to solve difficult problems even before they have learned the material.

- Students are allowed to explore topics of interest related to the content area.

- Students are assessed through assessments designed to focus on real-world applications.

- Students help determine how they demonstrate learning and how they are assessed.

Strategies for Assessing Prior Knowledge

Creating curiosity is the key to student engagement in the learning environment. How does one create curiosity in our adolescent learners? Allowing students to get a peek at what they will be learning, helping them realize that they already hold knowledge on a particular topic, or providing them with a forum for sharing their views will create this curiosity, which is the necessary ingredient for active social studies and history learning. Classroom strategies that assess prior knowledge through reflection and questioning will help create a classroom in which all students, including those with ADHD, will learn.

Anticipation Guides

Anticipation guides prepare students to learn new content by creating a purpose for their learning. A simple anticipation guide might consist of a single statement that students are asked to respond to—for example, "All cells are permeable." Students are then required to confer with a partner or within their group to come to consensus on an answer and a reason for their response. The results of this process allow the teacher to assess the level of understanding across the classroom. The brief discussion sets the stage for the learning that will occur. A more involved anticipation guide might use a series of statements that each student responds to individually before and after the lesson, the reading, or the unit. This type of anticipation guide supports the needs of students with ADHD because it provides a framework for the learning that will occur and allows students to use their own critical thinking skills to come up with reasons for their responses.

Scavenger Hunt

This pre-lesson assessment strategy supports students with ADHD who need to move around and allows the teacher to assess what students collectively know about the topic that will be discussed. A scavenger hunt contains several questions on a topic. Students are allowed to be the expert and answer one of the questions, but they must find other classmates or resources to answer the other questions on their scavenger hunt sheet. The number of questions depends on the level of assessment that the teacher wants to do and the time available. The benefit is that students get to interact and the questions guide the discussions between individuals. Again, this assessment benefits teachers by increasing their awareness of students' prior knowledge of the content but also creates a framework for student learning in the upcoming lesson.

Taking a Stand

This strategy for assessing prior knowledge combines an anticipation guide, movement, and cooperative learning. The teacher provides statements on the content that is going to be discussed on posters in different places in the classroom. Students are encouraged to "take a stand" under the poster that they agree with or that best describes their knowledge on the subject. Once students have assembled under a poster, they share why they agree with the statement or position. Together, the group develops a list of reasons for their stand that is shared with the whole class.

Give One, Get One

In this pre-lesson assessment strategy, students are able to share with each other what they already know about a certain topic. Students begin with a data collection sheet and write three responses to the question or prompt that include specific reasons or causes. Once all students have written down three responses of their own, they move about the room, giving one reason to another classmate while taking down data from another classmate. This process continues until the prescribed number of entries have been made. Once the data sheet is full, students can work in groups to prioritize or categorize the data they have collected. Students with ADHD have a chance to be actively involved in the process, and the data creates the advance organizer that will focus students on the topic of discussion.

K-W-L Charts

The Know–Want to know–Learned (K-W-L) chart is an advance organizer that is well known to most teachers and students. It is an effective tool for assessing prior knowledge because students list what they already know about the topic under the "K" column of the three-column chart. Students can fill out their own chart as well as write on sticky notes and affix them to a class chart. This process allows the teacher to very quickly assess what level of knowledge his students currently have. The "W" part lets students reflect on what they want to know about the topic. Reflection is essential in creating a purpose or meaning for the content being studied. If the student has questions on the topic, they will form the reason for the research that the student will do during all the activities and lessons related to the topic. Once a student has a personal connection, a desire to know something about the topic, he will be more likely to stay engaged in learning throughout the process. The "L" part of the chart is the living part of the chart that constantly changes as students learn and find the answers to the questions related to what they want to know. Again, if students have their own charts they can keep updating them as they learn new concepts, and a class chart with sticky note entries reinforces the idea that students are learning and finding the answers that they were looking for. This activity is intrinsically motivating when students see the list under the "L" grow much longer than the others.

Strategies for Direct Instruction

Direct instruction is essential in order for students with ADHD to acquire content knowledge. Without the structure of direct instruction, it is difficult for students with ADHD to determine what is important to learn, for they do not have the tools to systematically obtain this information on their own. In direct instruction, the teacher is the disseminator of information that provides the students with a pathway through the content. Instructional strategies that scaffold this process are necessary in order for your students to maneuver through complex ideas.

Advance Organizers

Like teachers of any other content area, teachers of science and social studies must provide all their students with the scaffolds needed to move them toward independent practice and application of learned skills. When teachers present new information, instructional scaffolding allows students to move just beyond their current level of skill or knowledge, into the *zone of proximal development* described by Vygotsky.[17] Scaffolding of new information and the use of such tools as advance organizers, guided notes, graphic organizers, pictures, charts, demonstrations, role playing, simulations, and other interactive strategies allow students to maneuver complex ideas within a provided structure. The sciences and social studies are ideal content areas in which to employ many of the essential strategies that facilitate student learning.

In addition, it is essential for students with ADHD who struggle with listening, comprehending, and taking notes at the same time to have the scaffold of an advance organizer in the form of guided notes or a graphic organizer of the essential information.[18] The advance organizer provides an intellectual framework in which discrete events are organized under larger ideas, themes, and generalizations.[19] These tools work well for students with ADHD because they focus the students' attention on large ideas and help them to organize the information learned via the lecture method.[20] Using advance organizers provides students with a structure for what they are to look for and listen for within the content of the lecture.

As students learn within their zone of proximal development, we know that initially the teacher will be doing all the modeling and the students will be simply following along in order to fill out the advance organizer. As the teacher moves from the "I do" stage to the "we do" stage, students will be able to fill out some of the guided notes with the teacher, making suggestions or working with partners to determine what part of the lecture information should go into the notes. It is not until students have had many opportunities to practice using advance organizers that the teacher will be able to expect that they will be able to determine, without support, the salient points of the lecture to put into their advance organizers. As with all other strategies, the more consistently and frequently the same strategies or routines are used, the more quickly students will move toward independent implementation of these strategies. The advance organizers shown in Figures 6.1 and 6.2 can be used to support students in identifying the main idea and the salient subsidiary points of a lecture. These graphic organizers of the important information can be used in place of note taking or in conjunction with note taking to provide an improved way to remember the information.

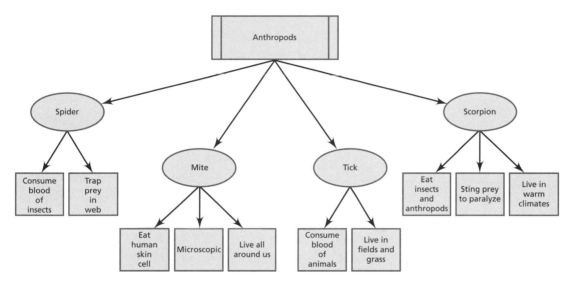

Figure 6.1: Example of an Advanced Organizer

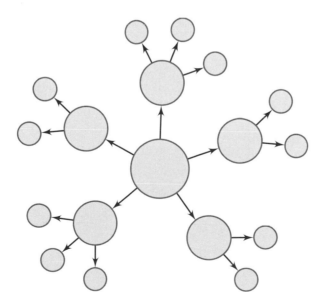

Figure 6.2: Another Advanced Organizer

Lectures

Although lectures have long been the norm in science and social studies classrooms across the country, more interactive teaching strategies are becoming more common. A variety of interactive strategies are discussed in this chapter, but the point should be made that at times, the teacher needs to be a disseminator of information and therefore there is a place for the direct instruction of lecture in science and social studies classrooms.

> A good lecture is concise, systematic, and sequential and provides information in an interesting way.

Lecture is most appropriate for introducing a unit, describing or presenting a problem for discussion, reviewing important concepts, providing information that cannot be obtained in any other way, and clarifying or re-teaching concepts when a need is identified through checks for understanding.[21] Good lectures do not meander and are directly related to the learning standard of the day. The best lectures are a response to the questions generated in the anticipatory set or the activities involved in assessing prior knowledge. A good lecture is concise, systematic, and sequential and provides information in an interesting way.

The information disseminated in a lecture is provided in chunks, with frequent stops for students to answer questions or respond to prompts either independently or in cooperative groups. Lecture sessions should follow the 10:2 rule, which calls for no more than ten minutes of instruction time to be followed by two minutes of checking for understanding or response. In addition, good lectures are always supported by visual media such as PowerPoint slides, SmartBoards, or multimedia presentations that address the attentional needs of students with ADHD.

Note Taking

Note taking is difficult for students with ADHD. As mentioned earlier, it is difficult for them to listen, process, and take notes at the same time[22]; therefore, scaffolds for note taking are essential. You may find that some of the students with ADHD in your classroom have Section 504 accommodations that pertain to note taking. These students often need a copy of the notes provided for them because they cannot grasp content when they try to take notes. Others may not have this accommodation, so note-taking scaffolds will be necessary. A variety of note-taking structures have been created by experts in student learning; the most frequently used are Cornell notes (see Figure 6.3).

Many other note-taking formats have been created and successfully used in different classrooms for different purposes. One model, the two-column format,

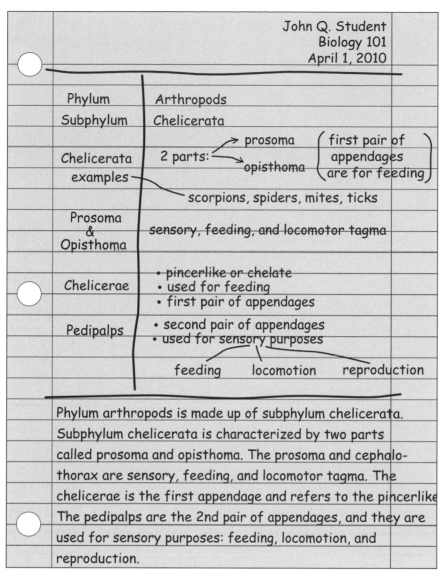

Figure 6.3: Cornell Notes

helps students see the visual distinction between main ideas and details and can be used for studying and as a scaffold for the development of summaries (see Figures 6.4 and 6.5). It is important to give students some time after note taking to solidify and organize ideas as well as forge connections to previously taught concepts.[23]

Moving students from dependence to independence may mean that initially the teacher will provide many of the key points already filled out on the advance organizer as a model or exemplar of what the important information might be. Students might initially only highlight those key points on their advance organizer when the teacher comes to those points in the lecture or discussion. Over time, students will recognize from the structure of the advance organizer and

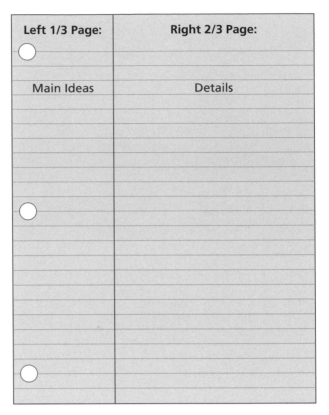

Left 1/3 Page:	Right 2/3 Page:
Main Ideas	Details

Figure 6.4: How to Take Two-Column Notes

from ongoing practice and consistency in the use of a specific organizer where the important information goes on the advance organizer and will be able to fill it out independently as they listen and follow along. As a teacher, you will find that some students move to this independent stage very quickly and that some students will continue to need the scaffold of visual support and modeling throughout the school year.

Strategies for Using Cooperative Groups

Cooperative grouping is an instructional strategy that can be effectively used in any content area. Due to the rich opportunities for research and discussion, science and social studies classes are a great place to use this strategy.

Numbered Heads Together

In the numbered-heads-together strategy, teachers assign each student a number. This can be done in a variety of ways. The simplest way is for students to count off to four or six or however large you want each group to be. Each group then contains one student with each number, and each group works together to come

Strategies for Teaching Adolescents with ADHD

Types of Fossils (Rock and Preserved)

Petrified	desc	• minerals replace all or part of the organism
	ex	• Petrified wood
Molds/casts		• the most common fossils
		• mold-hollow area in sediment in the shape of organism
		• cost-copy of the shape
Carbon films		• thin coating of carbon or rock in shape of organism
Trace		• Evidence of the activities of the organism
		• Footprint in rock
Amber		• hardend resin/sap
		• insects trapped • presening whole org.
Tar		• organism stuck in tar which preserves bones
		• La Brea tar pits-California
Ice		• Freezing preserves remains
		• Wooly Mammoth

Figure 6.5: An Example of Two-Column Notes

up with common agreements that the group can share with the class. Some teachers always have desks in groups of four and assign each desk a number, ensuring that there are always four students in each group. Other teachers may pass out cards with numbers to each student. As mentioned in previous chapters, teachers will find that students in groups are more productive when each student is given a specific assignment or role within the group. These assignments keep any one student from dominating the discussion and the group's work and keeps any student from letting the other students do the work for her. In numbered-heads groups, each person may play a different role but all are held accountable for the information because the teacher may call on any one of the members to share the group's response.

Jigsaw

In a jigsaw strategy, the content is divided into meaningful chunks, and then students within a cooperative group are counted off with numbers corresponding to each section of the content. Members of each home group each read the content independently and then meet with "experts" from other groups who have read the same content. In this expert group, they discuss what they have read and come to conclusions on how to best teach the content to their home group. They may need a scaffold of "expert sheets" or guiding questions to ensure that the salient points will be shared with the home group. After their expert meetings, students come back to their home group and each expert has the opportunity to teach the content to his group. Advance organizers or guided notes ensure that the home group records the correct information. This strategy allows the class to cover a large portion of science or social studies content in a relatively short amount of time.

Carousel Walk

A creative, interactive way to engage students with the content in a science or social studies lesson is to use a number of stations, with individual prompts at each. The teacher writes questions, posts problems, or provides historical documents for review at each station. Students move in groups around the room, responding to the questions, problems, or documents. The groups work to determine possible options for answers either on a poster with a colored marker or on sheets with guided notes. Each group is able to learn from the responses of the other groups in a discussion following the carousel walk. This process can be used as an anticipation guide, as a way to disseminate information, or as a review process to check for understanding. This strategy benefits students with ADHD because they can move around, talk about what they know, check their answers with their peers, and gain knowledge in ways other than through lectures or textbooks.

Strategies for Checking for Understanding

A variety of strategies besides quizzes and tests allow a teacher to check for understanding. Teachers can use active learning strategies to determine whether students have learned science or social studies content or whether re-teaching is necessary.

Summaries

Summaries are one way that students can convey what they know. While writing a summary is often a difficult assignment for students with ADHD who struggle with writing, it is a necessary skill for higher education, so scaffolding is necessary. Similar to the strategies discussed for math problem solving, a specific structure or checklist of steps will help a student with ADHD who struggles with the sequencing that is necessary to put a summary together.

Summary Writing Steps

1. Read the material and distinguish the main ideas from the details.

2. List the main ideas in phrase form.

3. Include a few details (only if necessary).

4. Combine the sentences into a paragraph.

5. Use transition words, and include a topic sentence.

Using the two-column note format, students can use the scaffold of the main ideas and details from the notes to put together a cohesive summary. The scaffold of transition words helps students who struggle with taking notes and putting them into sentences.[24]

Purpose	Transition Words
To list or present series:	First, second, next, finally
To indicate time order:	Before, after, since, later, eventually, at this time
To show cause & effect:	Therefore, because, as a result, consequently
To contrast an idea:	Yet, however, on the other hand
To add information:	Also, in addition, further
To summarize or conclude:	In conclusion, in other words, to sum up

Ticket to Leave

This process allows the teacher to quickly assess whether students have grasped the concepts of the lesson for the day. It is a quick formative assessment that circumvents the retrieval problems faced by many students with ADHD. The ticket is used at the end of an instructional period, when students write a summary or responses to questions on a slip of paper and hand it to the teacher when they leave the room. When teachers use these tickets as tools to monitor progress and assess student knowledge, students with ADHD do not have to access recall on a different date for that particular material. This process also lets the teacher know whether re-teaching is necessary and which students may need additional scaffolds.

Question-Answer Match

This strategy allows students to show what they know by matching question cards with answer cards. The matching can be done in a variety of ways that provide students with opportunities for cooperative learning and teachers with ways to assess knowledge. Teachers can provide the questions on an overhead or PowerPoint transparency and have sets of answer cards for each cooperative group of students. Each student is given an answer card or two. Group members come to consensus on the correct answer for each question and on the reason for their decision. The teacher may then use a numbered-head response to call on one student from each group to stand and share an answer and the reason for the answer. The other groups are required to agree or disagree with the group's response. Another option is for each group to have both the questions and the answers; students match them in the group, collectively determine the reasons for their decisions, and write these on a sheet of guided notes or another graphic organizer.

Chunking Tests

Summative assessments are still required in both science and social studies classes. Tests are often difficult for students with ADHD, not because they don't know the content but because they struggle with accessing recall. A teacher can provide scaffolds for summative assessments by chunking them into shorter, more frequent tests. Rather than waiting until the end of a unit to give the end-of-unit test, teachers can test each of the chapter sections as they are completed. The same content is assessed, but it is assessed in smaller chunks that are easier to recall. Students with ADHD will more likely be able to focus and sustain attention on these smaller chunks of information than on a large quantity of information that will seem overwhelming to study and hold in their memory.

In addition, the teacher can provide scaffolds within the structure of the test itself by providing visual breaks on the page. Creating word banks for fill-in-the-blank sections with only four to five questions in each section make taking the test much more doable than having twenty questions with a large word bank at the top or bottom of the page. Multiple-choice questions and a variety of other short-answer responses are more beneficial in determining what students with ADHD know than test items that require long essay-type answers.

When summative assessments focus on what students know rather than grades, teachers will find many creative strategies for assessing content knowledge other than tests from the textbook.

To Sum Up

Teachers of science and social studies who have students with ADHD in their classroom face the challenge of making history and science content real and applicable to all of their students. A student-centered classroom promotes instruction that keeps students intellectually engaged with the instruction. The research-based practices and strategies described in this chapter will provide you with tools that will help you in the endeavor of bringing history, government, and science alive for your students with ADHD.

Chapter 7

Creating a Positive Learning Environment for Students with ADHD

Moving from classroom to classroom as many as six or seven times a day can be an anxiety-producing experience for any student, but for your students with ADHD, 25 percent of whom suffer from anxiety disorders, school is not a place where they want to be! Teachers who are inconsistent in their classroom routines and expectations only make matters worse. Struggling with memory deficits, a student with ADHD is unsure of what each of his six bosses expects in each class and knows that, inevitably, somewhere in the course of the day, he will break one of the myriad of rules and individualized expectations and find himself in trouble. This alone may explain many of the common elusive headaches, stomach aches, and other ailments that students with ADHD come up with on any given school day.

For students with ADHD, a lack of structure, routine, or direction opens the door for their impulsivity to take control! In this mode, mistakes are inevitable, along with the punishment that follows. These students need structure, supervision, and direction from an adult. They need routines that limit their choices and decisions. For them, unstructured time in the day is a recipe for disaster.[1]

Teachers and schools can solve this problem by simply adopting a single set of rules and expectations for any and every classroom in the school.

> For students with ADHD, a lack of structure, routine, or direction opens the door for their impulsivity to take control!

When the expectations for each classroom are consistent, the student does not need to remember for each teacher what the entry procedure is, how and where to turn in homework, and what to do when starting class. When schoolwide routines are developed, along with schoolwide behavioral expectations, students with ADHD can put more of their working memory to work in learning the content rather than figuring out what each teacher expects of him.

The Research

While reactive behavior management has been the norm in schools for as long as schools have existed, the research has continued to support a change from reactive to proactive behavior management strategies. Unfortunately, despite the research, positive strategies are used sporadically in schools. To counteract these reactive approaches, teachers must be willing to release the autonomy of their own "kingdom" in their classroom and accept schoolwide behavioral expectations. When a school staff has identified the behaviors they want to see rather than the behaviors they don't want to see, appropriate behaviors are positively reinforced in a schoolwide, consistent manner. These common behavioral expectations provide the stability and consistency that students with ADHD need in order to successfully manage their behavior throughout the day.

Positive Behavior Supports

Much has been written on schoolwide positive behavior supports, yet they continue to be inconsistently utilized in schools today. For the most part, the lack of utilization comes back to the silo mentality that has ruled classrooms for the past century. Teachers have had the prerogative to create their own kingdom with their own set of rules and expectations with complete autonomy. This autonomy has been the norm and, without sweeping change, will continue to be the norm, but this philosophy alone reduces the chances for behavioral and academic success for students with ADHD.

The benefits of developing a positive school climate through positive behavior support include maximizing academic engagement and achievement, minimizing rates of rule-violating behaviors, creating an environment in which school functions are organized more efficiently and effectively, and creating improved support for students with disabilities, including those with ADHD and others at risk for educational failure.[2]

Practices That Don't Work

Identifying current or previous practices that don't work is one way to begin the process of developing a new, more positive approach to creating an effective school climate. Although zero-tolerance policies are necessary for extremely dangerous infractions such as possession of a weapon or drugs, the get-tough policy in most schools has not improved either behavior or academic outcomes. Get-tough policies often include clamping down on behaviors and increased supervision and monitoring. The unfortunate result of this type of policy is that it fosters an environment of control rather than of cooperation, and it triggers and reinforces antisocial behavior, shifts accountability away from the school and onto the student, and extremely devalues the student-adult relationship.[3] The interventions employed in this kind of reactive policy usually involve removing a student and assigning responsibility for change to someone else. Even though these detention practices don't seem to work, increased surveillance continues, and increases rather than reductions in suspensions and expulsions usually result. This systemic response just fosters the notion that these kids are bad and that they will only respond to even more aversive strategies. Despite the research on positive behavior supports that does not support this ineffective approach to behavior management, these practices are still widely used.

> The get-tough policy in most schools has not improved either behavior or academic outcomes.

Practices That *Do* Work

To counteract the reactive approach to behavior management, it is essential to come to a common belief about students. First, they are not born with bad behaviors, and second, they do not learn new appropriate behaviors through continual aversive consequences. They learn better ways of behaving when they are taught directly and receive frequent positive feedback on their development of prosocial behaviors.

Positive behavior supports are not specific practices or something that can be bought in a box, but rather a general approach to preventing problem behavior. This approach is not limited to a specific type of student, but is an approach to be used with all students in all classrooms, covering schoolwide and classroom-wide management systems, individual classroom management, behavioral expectations for specific settings and events, and individual student-specific systems.[4]

In building schoolwide and classroom-wide systems, school teams establish common approaches and purposes for the behavioral expectations that they develop. Within this

> Positive behavior supports are not specific practices or something that can be bought in a box, but rather a general approach to preventing problem behavior.

structure, they define exactly what they expect behaviorally from students, using positive language. They determine when and how they will directly teach these behavioral expectations and what they will do to reinforce them, as well as what they will do to deter inappropriate behaviors. They also implement a schoolwide system that will monitor and evaluate the new system. Monitoring is essential in order to determine whether the system that has been developed is effective and whether it is producing the outcome of positive behavior development that was intended.

The teacher reinforces these schoolwide collaborative decisions and behavioral expectations by teaching and practicing the agreed-on behaviors in the classroom until the students can quickly and easily explain them and can be observed participating in them without reminders. This teacher makes a commitment to implement "behavior boot camp" for the first few weeks of school and continues to practice and model these behavioral routines and expectations whenever it becomes apparent that the students need more practice.[5]

> If teachers do not take the time to teach behavioral expectations at the beginning of the school year, they will be dealing with behavior all year long. They will spend the year "chasing the cows" because they were too busy to build the fence.

The teacher also makes a commitment to use five positives for each negative response. Teachers who take this task seriously may want to write the word "Positive" on their back wall, so that they can see it each time they face the class as a reminder that each time the class is addressed, using a positive statement first will produce a more timely and positive response from the students.

Teachers have the ability to change a classroom from a negative environment to a positive one by redirecting behavior and being proactive in their approaches to typical student behaviors. In order to manage behaviors proactively rather than reactively, teachers must have the skill to anticipate problems and difficulties that may occur. These teachers recognize during planning and during instruction when behavior can go awry. They have a plan in place to deal with that behavior. During instruction, they recognize that moving toward the student or student group that is potentially going to have difficulty may stop the difficulty before it starts. Proactive teachers recognize situations between students and distract them with a job or chore. Lee Canter identifies proactive teachers as those who anticipate misbehavior and plan in advance how to deal with it in a positive manner.[6] On the other hand, reactive discipline is defined as waiting until a student misbehaves and then determining what to do to get her back on course.

Behavioral experts suggest some of the following strategies to support proactive rather than reactive behavior management.

Proactive Discipline Ideas

- Provide an agenda for each period so that students are clear on what to expect.

- Provide classroom structure and routine that supports students with ADHD and other weaknesses in executive functions.

- Provide clear, concise instructions on what the expectations are for each activity of the day.

- Explicitly review behavioral expectations prior to activities, providing examples and non-examples. Have students orally repeat directions back several times to ensure that they have a clear understanding of the expectations.

- Verbally reinforce appropriate behavior whenever possible. A simple "Thank you for following directions" goes a long way in reinforcing appropriate behaviors. All students essentially want to please their teachers. When you recognize their attempts, they will be highly likely to continue trying to please you.

- Reward direction, not perfection. When students attempt to improve their behavior, it is important to recognize their efforts even when the target behavior has not yet been perfectly achieved. Encouraging their attempts will increase the likelihood that they will continue to work toward the desired behavior.

- Anticipate problems and difficulties by preparing students for changes and transitions during the class period.

- Distract or redirect a student from being disruptive; call on her to do a task or help solve a problem.

- Use a signal to get all the students' attention such as a bell or a flick of the lights. This alone may stop inappropriate behaviors.

- When disruptions are brewing, move closer to a student. This "proximity control" is sometimes enough to stop behavior without any verbal warnings or instruction.

- When a student begins to get involved in a disruption, sending him to a non-punitive exile can be very effective. Have him take a note to the office or some books to the library.

- Specifically telling students what you want them to do, not what you *don't* want them to do, will change behavior. Telling a student "Keep your eyes on me" is a better directive than "Stop looking at her!" If students perceive that they are doing something, they are less likely to misbehave.

A positive classroom is an environment that is built on positive reinforcement; positive behaviors are recognized and reinforced.[7] This environment is built on the premise that positive reinforcement changes behavior, whereas negative reinforcement only stops behavior.[8] Positively reinforcing the behavior that the teacher wants increases the likelihood that the behavior will occur again.[9]

> Positive reinforcement changes behavior, whereas negative reinforcement only stops behavior.

Positive, proactive teachers also recognize that certain activities or situations may need additional instruction and behavioral support. They recognize that not all students respond to their positive behavior strategies and that those students may need additional or secondary support. The only way a teacher can determine the need for additional support for a student with ADHD is to monitor the student's behaviors. Many teachers have felt that "that kid" is always off task and disrupting the class, but when a teacher focuses on specific behaviors that are defined as off task or disruptive and then keeps a tally, he may find that the behavior only *seems* to be happening all the time. Monitoring behavior is essential to an effective positive behavior management process.

Students with ADHD will struggle with behavior in class, so it is essential to keep track of specific behaviors and the frequency of their occurrence. If a student is disruptive a specific number of times a day or is sent out of class a certain number of times, it is essential that the classroom teacher request support for managing this behavior. Secondary behavior supports are explored later in this chapter, but without data, it is difficult for those involved to be able to recognize what the behavior is communicating or how to meet the need that the behavior is calling attention to.

Many students with ADHD will need secondary support to meet their specific behavioral challenges, but effective teachers, armed with the right tools, can make a significant impact on the behavior of students with ADHD, keeping them from needing the secondary or intensive behavioral interventions often associated with ADHD.

Preventing Problem Behaviors

When teachers collaboratively develop clear rules and expectations that are implemented schoolwide, they need to keep in the forefront of their planning and decision making the development of socially appropriate interpersonal skill development. The schoolwide rules should not focus on compliance alone, but should be developed in order to help students build the appropriate skills to become better citizens.[10] Developing young adults who can problem solve to work through disagreements by directly teaching them appropriate choice-making skills will help them in all aspects of their adult lives. This opportunity to teach socially appropriate behavior is of primary importance in our society, where collaboration skills are key to career success.

Beginning with Respect

Recognizing that students deserve respect is the first step in developing a positive classroom climate. If students are treated with disdain and are belittled on a daily basis, they will not have any intrinsic desire to please the person who is demeaning them. Most schools that use punitive measures to bring students into compliance routinely treat students with disdain and a lack of respect. It should not surprise the administration that behavior does not change, despite all the punitive measures used at a school site. Even the most difficult of all students do well for the few teachers who treat them with respect. These teachers are not soft, nor do they let students do whatever they want. This is not respect. Respect is treating a student the way you as a teacher and adult would like to be treated. Showing respect involves basic manners, such as saying "thank you" and "please." Recognizing the needs of a student and affirming him and his needs is all it takes to let him know that you recognize him as a person and respect the person that he is.

Realizing that a student with ADHD has difficulties with monitoring and self-regulating her behavior, you show her respect when you consult with her to develop a silent signal or prompt that does not draw attention to her, but reminds her that she is off task. This signal might be as simple as walking by and putting your hand on her desk or standing next to her desk while you continue talking. This type of prompt will not draw attention to her, but will help her realize when she needs to monitor herself and bring herself back to the group.

In addition, recognizing that a student with ADHD is getting restless and needs a motor break rather than just trying to ignore it is another sign of respect and understanding. This motor break can be something for the whole class to do, like moving to get books or materials or taking a planned motor break—for example, moving to stations that will help all students—or the break can be specifically for that student—for example, you might ask him to run an errand for you, retrieve supplies or materials, collect papers, or perform some other activity that will allow him to move and release some of his pent-up energy. In highly engaging student-centered classrooms, movement is usually built into the regular classroom routine, so extra motor breaks are rarely required.

Understanding the Issue of Fairness

Treating students with respect and creating a fair and safe learning environment does not mean that everyone is treated exactly the same. This distinction is key in the recognition that the students in your classroom with ADHD may need some unequal treatment in order to truly be treated fairly. To be able to implement this truth, it is important to recognize that fair and equal are not the same. Most of us equate these two words because they have similar meanings, but *fair* and *equal* are not the same.[11] It is hard for some teachers to embrace this idea, and they may feel like they are cheating when they allow their student with ADHD extra directions, open notes, or extra time. Some teachers feel that allowing a student with ADHD some accommodation is not fair because all the other students do not get the same accommodation. At this point, it is essential to understand that treating the student equally would not mean that the student with ADHD would have the same learning experience as her peers. She has a disability; they do not. It is in the law that accommodations written into the IEP or 504 plan must be provided. No questions about fair or equal can change the rights of a student with a disability.

Teachers who personally agree that fairness may require different treatment for students with ADHD and other disabilities may still be reluctant to implement these accommodations because they are concerned that other students will complain about the perceived inequality. This is a legitimate concern, but most students will understand that some students need different treatment. They can understand that not all students need glasses to be treated fairly, so in the same way, not all students need additional time, a quiet work space, open notes, or the use of a computer to be treated fairly. A simple explanation is usually enough.

> It is important to recognize that fair and equal are not the same.

Sticking to Rituals and Routines

Provide direct instruction on daily rituals and routines. This instruction should include entry procedures, exit procedures, homework procedures, and how to move around the room, ask for help, turn in papers, use the rest room, get a tissue, and so on. Students need to know what is expected from the moment they enter the room. This routine should remain the same each day of the school year. Having a routine means that the teacher must *always* have a warm-up exercise on the board or screen when students enter the room, that the agenda and homework is *always* posted and in the same place. This type of routinized classroom is one of the strategies that will help students with ADHD find success. When students understand that from day to day, the order of activities, the specific routine for each activity, and the behavioral expectations for each activity remain the same, they will learn through repetition to follow the routines and will be able to comply with behavioral and academic expectations through daily practice.

Providing Clear and Concise Instructions

Another strategy that helps students with ADHD is giving specific directions, naming exactly what you want students to do—for example, "Everyone take out your math notebook." The next direction would not be given until *all* students have complied with the first one, providing time for students to comply. Once the first action has been completed, students would be given the next direction—for example, "Copy the problem of the day into your notebook." This *chunking* of directions into small parts helps students who have difficulties with following multi-step directions due to distractibility and short-term memory deficits.[12] Mel Levine reports that short-term memory provides very brief retention, usually two seconds for new information. Short-term memory allows information into working memory in chunks, where most children recode it into chunks. Children with attentional issues may not be paying attention to the most important chunks of information and find that they are lost.

Ensuring that all students are attending when you are giving directions is another essential strategy for helping students with ADHD in your classroom. Using a signal such as a bell, chime, or music or a visual cue such as flicking the lights ensures that all students are attending before you give directions. Waiting until *all* students are attending is another important engagement strategy. For some students with ADHD, it is the silence before the directions that grabs their attention, so waiting for all to be quiet before giving directions helps them to focus.

Giving mandatory instructions using the word *everyone* and waiting until all have complied also gives the sense that no one is allowed to not be paying attention. In addition, having several students repeat the directions makes it more likely that a student with ADHD will catch at least one of the iterations of the directions. Writing the gist of the directions on bullet points on the board also helps students who waver in and out of attending.

Maintaining a Perky Pace

Anita Archer, a well-known public speaker on differentiated instructional strategies and instructional scaffolds, recognizes that teaching at a "perky pace" is an effective strategy for keeping students engaged. A brisk pace creates an atmosphere of energy or perhaps even urgency that keeps students focused and alert. Because students with ADHD struggle to remain focused, it is essential to use a quick pace in the classroom in order to keep their attention and thus improve their learning.

Using a timer like the Time Timer during instruction is one way to ensure that the pace stays perky.[13] Teachers who give students a four-minute time limit to copy and answer the problem of the day will find that their students get to work immediately. They will find that there is less time spent looking for pens and papers and chitchatting simply due to the fact that a time limit has been given. Some teachers use a timer on the overhead projector that shows the seconds counting down so that students are acutely aware of the passage of time and their need to get busy. Of course, we realize that students with ADHD process more slowly, so a check-in at the end of four minutes to see whether anyone needs more time is an essential accommodation, but the use of a timer alone will increase on-task behavior. Teachers who use timers also realize that they stay on track better, cover more material during the period, and do not let students get them off on a tangent, nor can one student distract the teacher for personal help for too long when a timer is in use. Challenging students to beat the clock is another very effective strategy for secondary school students.

Analyzing Problem Behaviors

Reactive behavior management can only be extinguished when both teachers and students take the time to analyze problem behaviors. Impulsive students with ADHD who struggle with emotional regulation will find simply stopping behaviors to be an impossible task. They need to be given the gift of opportunities for reflection in order to try to recognize patterns in their own behaviors and determine why they occur. This type of reflection requires the perspective of a nonemotional observer and ongoing hard data on the behaviors to help both the student and the teacher recognize and ultimately change problem behaviors. Recognizing how to analyze these behaviors will allow you to be an effective change agent in helping students overcome their behavioral difficulties.

What Is the Behavior Communicating?

Having ADHD is not a "get out of jail free" card[14]; students with ADHD are responsible for their behavior, even though they may have a difficult time controlling it. In order for students to learn self-regulating behaviors, it is essential that they begin to understand what causes them to misbehave. Once she is caught in an emotion, such understanding is essentially impossible for the student. Only after the emotion has passed can the behavior truly be analyzed.

Although consequences must be enforced, it is important to try to look at behavior patterns in a non-punitive way. The student already feels bad for losing control when it happened; he does not need the past dredged up again when the behavior is being analyzed. The purpose of the analysis is to determine what the behavior is communicating. What are the mitigating factors that are leading to the behavior? Only through careful monitoring of the

Strategies for Teaching Adolescents with ADHD

behavior over time can both you and the student begin to recognize the patterns that lead to the behavior.

Analyzing the behavior requires a non-emotional observer's perspective. Rather than seeing the behavior as an affront to you and your authority in the classroom, you need to work with the student. Looking at why the behavior occurs is the only way that the student will be able to gain control over it. As the behavior is monitored over time, some patterns will begin to emerge. As you analyze the patterns, you and the student can try to determine the answers to the following questions: What happened right before the behavioral outburst? Does this type of outburst occur around the same time each day? Does it always happen around another student? Does it happen during certain parts of the class—for example, group work, independent work, warm-ups, or some other activity? Do behavioral issues only happen in one class or period of the day? Analyzing the situation will often reveal to both you and the student the real reason for the ongoing behavior.[15] Analyzing the behavior helps the student recognize where the danger areas are and what activities might lead to behavioral problems. This understanding helps the student develop his self-regulation skills. Guiding the student in the analysis of his behavior and helping him identify ways to change those behaviors is a gift beyond measure. Behavior usually has a purpose; helping the student identify it will go a long way toward helping him overcome the challenges that result from his weaknesses in modulating emotions and self-regulating his behavior.

As you and the student analyze his behaviors, you will often find that the behavior is intended to cover up some academic deficit. Many students would rather be viewed as bad than dumb any day![16] For this reason, it is important to observe whether misbehavior or significant off-task behavior is occurring only during specific instructional times in your classroom. The student may be acting out in order to cover up his inability to follow directions or complete a task or to avoid divulging that he has forgotten his work again. Students may act out just so that they can be removed from class and the potentially embarrassing situation. This option is often preferable to being embarrassed in front of their peers.

Why Doesn't She Ask for Help?

Students with ADHD and learning disabilities rarely ask for help in class. This reticence is puzzling to many teachers, but it is due to the fact that these students have difficulties with forming questions. This weakness in interrogation leaves students unable to get the help that they need.[17] In response, students will sit and do nothing, act disinterested in the work or simply find other things to do rather than get started. When you analyze this behavior, you and the student may find that this behavior only occurs when independent practice begins and does not occur when assignments are done with cooperative groups. Continuing the analysis will help both you and the student to realize that the cause is not an inability to do the work but difficulty with getting started on something new without direct support. This behavior might look like a lack of motivation, a lack of focus, or outright defiance, but after your analysis, you will both be clear that it is not laziness but rather confusion about what the task entails and the inability to ask how to do it.

An effective solution might include standing near the student when reviewing directions or allowing the student to work with a partner through the first few tasks on all independent work. Briefly checking in and redirecting her if she is wrong will ensure that she understands what the task entails without making her ask for help. Once you are sure that she is on the right track, you can simply make a few sweeps to ensure that she is still on the right track. Why is it important to provide this support in getting started? Anxiety and difficulty in prioritizing and activating work are some causes of the behaviors that often disrupt class. Reducing anxiety and helping students get started will provide you with calmer and more on-task behavior in your classroom.

Research to Practice

As a classroom teacher, you have been faced with a myriad of behaviors from the first moment of the first day of school. How a teacher deals with these behaviors is usually what makes or breaks him or her. Teachers who have a strong understanding of positive behavior supports will implement consistent behavioral expectations from day one, but what happens when positive supports are not enough? Schools that understand the behavioral needs of all students have multiple tiers of behavioral interventions and supports in place as part of a schoolwide Response to Intervention (RtI) process (see Figure 7.1). These multiple tiers reflect the philosophy of a Response to Intervention model in which targeted behavioral support is provided to students at the level that they need to be successful. The tiers provide students with primary intervention, which is a schoolwide system for all staff, students, and settings; secondary intervention, which focuses on specialized groups who are at risk for misbehavior; and tertiary intervention, which is specialized and focuses on systems for individual students.[18]

Tier I: Primary Interventions

When a school implements a schoolwide positive behavior plan, they usually put in place multiple tiers of behavioral intervention to support the behavioral needs of all students. Primary interventions usually involve schoolwide rules that have been identified and explicitly taught, implementation of strategies to provide feedback and recognition for appropriate behaviors, and instructional practices that are engaging and actively involve all students. These strategies are implemented in all settings and include all students. In most cases, approximately

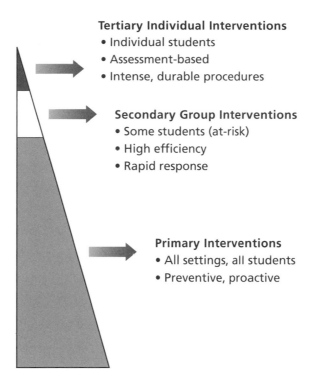

Tertiary Individual Interventions
- Individual students
- Assessment-based
- Intense, durable procedures

Secondary Group Interventions
- Some students (at-risk)
- High efficiency
- Rapid response

Primary Interventions
- All settings, all students
- Preventive, proactive

Figure 7.1: Multi-Tiered Behavioral Interventions

72 percent of the secondary school population need only the supports provided in this preventive, proactive behavioral tier.[19] These are the students who believe that the rules pertain to them.

Tier II: Secondary Group Interventions

Schoolwide supports for positive behavior provide a comprehensive, systematic plan that meets the behavioral needs of the majority of students.[20] While the schoolwide positive behavior plan meets the needs of the majority, approximately 22 percent of the secondary school population will need additional behavioral support.[21] This group often includes students with ADHD who still struggle with self-regulation and control, even with the support of the schoolwide structures. For this group of students, a secondary level of behavioral intervention should be made available before moving toward more intensive behavior supports. These secondary interventions usually require minimal time to implement and are very similar from student to student. Secondary interventions typically provide extra doses of positive supports.[22] These strategies usually include an increase in daily structure and organizational support, provision of more frequent behavioral prompts, and frequent doses of praise for appropriate behaviors.

One example of a secondary intervention is the Check In Check Out (CICO) process, also known as the Behavior Education Program.[23] It is a schoolwide intervention that all staff participate in and can be used for any student, including one with ADHD. The intervention is targeted at students who are regularly involved in low-level disruptive behaviors such as blurting out, irregular work completion, tardiness, and off-task behavior, which are frequent problem areas for students with ADHD.

The CICO process incorporates several core principles of positive behavior support:

1. Clearly defined expectations
2. Instruction on appropriate social skills
3. Increased positive reinforcement for following expectations
4. Contingent consequences for problem behavior
5. Increased positive contact with an adult at school
6. Improved opportunities for self-management
7. Increased home-school collaboration[24]

One of the most important benefits for adolescents is the increase in positive contact with adults at school. In comprehensive high schools today, students can go through an entire day without ever talking to another human being. For a young person with ADHD who suffers from anxiety, depression, and shortcomings in social skills, along with an inability to self-regulate behavior, each day of school can be torture. These students can walk through the day and remain totally disconnected. The CICO process allows them to forge a one-on-one relationship with at least one adult.

A student in the CICO program checks in with his designated adult at the beginning of each school day. This check-in is a catalyst for change; the student realizes that at least one adult cares about him and how he will make it through his day. During the check-in, expectations for behavior are reviewed, self-management strategies are developed, and a daily monitoring sheet is provided (see Figure 7.2). The adult can help proactively trouble-shoot some common issues for young people with ADHD by checking to see whether the student has his homework, has his materials, and is ready for class.

At regular time intervals—usually at the beginning or end of each period—the student gets feedback on the target behavior. At the end of the day, the student checks out with the same adult by reviewing the monitoring sheet and determining whether behavioral goals were met. The data is charted, and the adult provides acknowledgment, encouragement, and a sense of caring. This same information is sent to parents at home.[25]

The daily data is compiled into weekly charts so that the student can analyze his behavior in order to identify strengths and needed improvements and determine whether there are any patterns related to behavioral difficulties. This ongoing monitoring and data analysis helps the student develop the self-management skills to

Check-In/Check-Out Daily Progress Report

Student's Name _____   Date _____

Teachers: Please use the following rubric to reflect student's progress on the following goals:

Mostly (5)   *Sometimes (3)*   *Never (1)*

Goals	1			2			3			4			5			6		
On Time	5	3	1	5	3	1	5	3	1	5	3	1	5	3	1	5	3	1
Prepared for Class	5	3	1	5	3	1	5	3	1	5	3	1	5	3	1	5	3	1
Followed Directions	5	3	1	5	3	1	5	3	1	5	3	1	5	3	1	5	3	1
Completed Tasks	5	3	1	5	3	1	5	3	1	5	3	1	5	3	1	5	3	1
Respectful to Others	5	3	1	5	3	1	5	3	1	5	3	1	5	3	1	5	3	1
TOTAL POINTS																		
TEACHER'S INITIALS																		

Daily Goal: (30–150)   Daily Score: (30–150)

Student Signature _____
Provide brief comments or observations:

Period 1 _____

Period 2 _____

Period 3 _____

Period 4 _____

Period 5 _____

Period 6 _____

Parent/Guardian Signature _____

Parent/Guardian Comments _____

Figure 7.2: Check-In/Check-Out Daily Progress Report

Chart created by Fred DeRuvo.

take greater responsibility for his own behavior. Over time, the process moves from a teacher-managed system to a student-managed system in which the student is able to monitor behavior independently.

Students with ADHD benefit greatly from this type of secondary intervention. With adequate support from teachers, many students will not need further specific interventions, and support for them can be gradually faded.

Tier III: Tertiary Individual Interventions

Students with ADHD often fall into the 5–10 percent of the student population that require more intensive tertiary interventions. Tertiary interventions involve an individualized assessment followed by development of an individualized intervention plan. A behavior specialist helps the student identify the function that the behavior fulfills—that is, how exhibiting the behavior helps the student get what he wants. Determining the function of the behavior is the first step in figuring out how to replace it. According to Sarah Fairbanks and her colleagues, most of these function-based interventions include providing more teacher attention, improving the student's self-monitoring skills, directly teaching social skills, breaking tasks down into smaller parts to reduce task duration, and giving the student scheduled breaks in order to work with adults or peers.[26] Another effective strategy in these plans is interspersing instruction between preferred activities. All these interventions can provide direct support for students with ADHD who have difficulties with executive functions related to sustaining attention to tasks, sustaining effort, modulating emotions, and monitoring and self-regulating actions.

As a classroom teacher, you may be involved in providing support for a student in a Tier II intervention, but typically Tier III interventions are developed by a team of school specialists that usually include a school psychologist or a school counselor. You will play a role in providing the classroom structure and reinforcement needed for the student to be able to change her behavior, but the plan will be developed by a team of professionals. You will help the student by providing the clear expectations, positive feedback and regard, and classroom instructional strategies that lead to active learning and student engagement.

To Sum Up

For students with ADHD, the struggle to maintain consistent, appropriate behavior is ongoing. Weaknesses in the executive functions involved in activating work, focusing attention, modulating emotions, sustaining effort, and self-regulating can lead the student down the road to negative school experiences. Research shows that schools and teachers can create an environment in which the blows of these weaknesses are softened. Students can make their way through the day successfully when they are provided with a positive, safe, and predictable environment. Given the struggles that these students face, it is our responsibility as educators to do whatever we can to provide them with the safety and security of a positive learning experience. The strategies offered in this chapter give you the tools to do just that.

Chapter 8

Working Together to Promote Postsecondary Success

While school is difficult for students with ADHD due to executive function deficits and the accompanying academic problems, the future is starting to look brighter. Historically, schools have had little awareness of or sympathy for the challenges these students face. As we realize that ADHD is not a willful behavioral disorder but truly a hidden disability that affects not just behavior but also learning, schools are becoming more attuned to the needs of these students. A greater understanding of your students with ADHD and your implementation of active learning strategies can be the catalyst that opens the doors to postsecondary educational goals for these students.

In this book, we have covered what ADHD may look like in your secondary school classroom. We have delved into general research-based instructional strategies that focus on meeting the needs of all students, including those with varied learning styles, and have looked specifically at content-based instructional strategies that have proven effective in teaching students with ADHD. We have focused almost primarily on you, the teacher, your instruction, and your behavior management practices. In this chapter, we will take a look at broader school-based interventions

> A greater understanding of your students with ADHD and your implementation of active learning strategies can be the catalyst that opens the doors to postsecondary educational goals for these students.

as well as the individual student's responsibility for achieving academic success and moving toward postsecondary education.

Responsibilities of the School

The school is responsible for educating all of its students in a safe learning environment. The implementation of NCLB has provided the impetus for schools to address the specific needs of all students on a campus, and does not allow schools to simply let students who have not acquired basic skills to continue to move on. Schools are required to provide instruction that allows each student to reach proficiency on state assessments. Although intervention is not written into NCLB, it is a by-product of the disaggregation of the scores of all learners, including students with disabilities, English learners, and students of low socioeconomic background.

Many schools and districts across the country have responded to the proficiency mandate by implementing numerous interventions to support their underperforming students. In the past, the practice has too often been that if a student struggled academically or did not grasp concepts in the same manner or at the same rate as his peers, he was referred to special education. With skyrocketing special education numbers, it became apparent that special education was becoming a dumping ground for at-risk and underperforming students.

Response to Intervention: Schoolwide Support for *All* Students

Response to Intervention (RtI) is a response to the practice of dumping students into special education. IDEA 2004 states that a student cannot qualify for special education services under the Specific Learning Disability category if she has not had appropriate instruction or access to quality instruction. The law also states that a multidisciplinary team can use a process that determines whether the student responds to scientific research-based interventions as part of the evaluation process concerning special education qualification. It is important to note that RtI is not just about special education qualification but is also about the prevention of academic failure and intervention on behalf of students who are at risk for failure.

Three Tiers of Academic Interventions

Response to Intervention is a systematic method of instruction and assessment of students.[1] RtI provides multiple levels of instruction and intervention that are based on student need as determined by universal screening and progress monitoring (see Figure 8.1). The first tier includes universal instruction and assessment of all

Strategies for Teaching Adolescents with ADHD

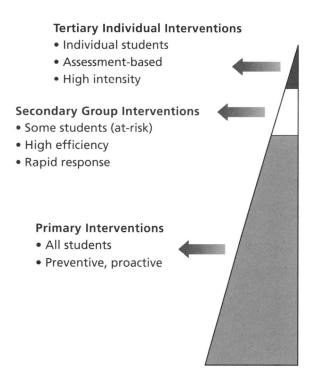

Tertiary Individual Interventions
• Individual students
• Assessment-based
• High intensity

Secondary Group Interventions
• Some students (at-risk)
• High efficiency
• Rapid response

Primary Interventions
• All students
• Preventive, proactive

Figure 8.1: The Three Tiers of Instruction in Response to Intervention

students. This level is about good "first teaching," using many of the student-centered active learning strategies discussed in this book so far. With good differentiated instruction, 80 percent of the typical students in a classroom will not need any additional scaffolds to meet content standards.

> The first tier includes universal instruction and assessment of all students. This level is about good "first teaching."

Students who have not met the standards through Tier I instruction need additional support. An example of Tier II instruction is an additional thirty minutes of daily instruction that is targeted to address a student's specific area of weakness. Tier II interventions prove most effective when intervention groups are small and homogeneous and the instruction is direct and strategy-based. Tier II instruction occurs for a specified period of time, and progress is monitored in an ongoing, systematic manner. If a student does not make progress toward proficiency during the Tier II intervention, a second intervention is often applied, using different strategies, for a specified amount of time.

If a student does not respond to the Tier II interventions, the school will provide more intensive intervention at Tier III. This intensive intervention includes an increase in instructional time and intervention in an even smaller group. Progress is monitored more frequently, and these data often become part of a comprehensive special education evaluation if the student does not respond to the intensity of the Tier III intervention. At this point, a multidisciplinary team will look specifically at why a student's performance is significantly different from that of other students of her age and grade and determine what additional special education supports she may need.[2]

Response to Intervention does not specifically focus on students with ADHD, but often these students fall into the at-risk category of students at a school site and are in need of additional instructional time or targeted intervention in Tiers II or III. Their ADHD symptoms do not warrant a special education evaluation, but accommodations from a 504 plan are not enough to support the student toward proficiency. These students benefit from additional targeted instruction in small-group settings that focus on strategy instruction that will help them with memory, recall, and problem solving.

> Response to Intervention does not specifically focus on students with ADHD, but often these students fall into the at-risk category of students.

RtI is an important schoolwide intervention because it ensures that all students have equal educational opportunity. It provides a mechanism whereby students can get the extra help that they need through supplementary instruction without stigmatizing special education labels. Schoolwide intervention provides an additional safety net for students with ADHD without drawing additional attention to their disability, given that the interventions are available to all students.

Collaboration: An Essential Component

There are numerous benefits to students, teachers, schools, and families when Response to Intervention processes are implemented. Students receive help as soon as the need is discovered. Students with ADHD can receive additional instructional help without needing a special education qualification. Parents can be relieved that their child is receiving extra help based on his needs, and teachers find that the collaboration that is inherent in an RtI structure provides them with an opportunity to solve problems with a team of their colleagues.

Essential to an RtI structure is ongoing collaborative time in which the team evaluates whether the instruction being provided is sufficient to ensure that students are meeting the standards. This collaborative process allows teachers to share the workload with a content and grade-level team. Teachers find that they can share strategies, materials, lessons, and approaches that have worked with their students, especially students who need a little extra attention, like those with ADHD. Schools that implement effective collaboration find that their teaching teams are working smarter and not harder and are able to work more specifically on the instructional needs of individual students in their instructional planning so that there is a greater chance that all students will succeed.

The collaborative process gives these teams a chance to learn from each other's best practices and improve the educations outcomes for all of their students.

Good teaching is the result. But where do the responsibilities of the family and the student lie in meeting the standards and expectations of the content and grade level?

Responsibilities of the Family

Although adolescents are on the path to independence, their family continues to play a great role in the life of teens with ADHD. While transitions are difficult for any student, students with ADHD need additional support through the typical transitions of school life. Chapter Seven discussed the difficulties associated with making the transition from elementary school to middle school. Students with ADHD, who have often been successful with the support of a single teacher in a multiple-subject classroom, may suddenly find themselves falling apart under the expectations of multiple teachers. The transition to high school is no easier; students must move into a larger and more unstructured environment. Students need to learn self-advocacy skills in order to navigate these transitions successfully, but it is also important to realize that for students with ADHD, parental support will often need to continue to a greater degree than it would for typically developing peers.

> Students with ADHD need additional support through the typical transitions of school life.

Parental Monitoring

Teachers need to recognize that the frequent monitoring of students by their parents is not intended to be an annoyance. These parents realize that checking on homework, assignments, test scores, and grades is a proactive strategy to make sure that their child with ADHD does not fall behind or suddenly receive failing grades. Teachers often think that by high school, students should be doing this monitoring on their own. For the student with ADHD, this is an important task to learn, but when the ultimate goal is graduating, parents realize that their intervention and monitoring is a necessary process that they hope will eventually be adopted by their child. Until then, it is essential to the success of these students that teachers collaborate and communicate with parents.

Medication: A Family and Student Decision

While many teachers would advocate that medicating students with ADHD would improve their classroom behavior and academic outcomes, it is imperative that teachers understand that the issue of medication is a family decision. By the time that students with ADHD have reached middle school and high school, most will already have a diagnosis in place. In many cases, these students will currently be taking medication or will have taken it in the past. Many schools have parents provide information about students' medications on the emergency card that is filled out before the student attends school. If you have concerns about medication and are not comfortable approaching the family on this issue at first, the emergency card will provide that important information. If the student is on medication, it is important to communicate with the parents if you are concerned about the student's behavior or academics, for the teacher's feedback is a helpful way for the family to determine the effectiveness of treatment with the medication.

While studies have shown that using medication is the single most important intervention that parents can make in managing a child's core ADHD symptoms,[3] many families and adolescents opt out of medication treatment, for a variety of reasons. Adolescents are in the stage of human development when they are trying to discover their true identity. This period of development is characterized by an ongoing effort to develop their own sense of self. Many adolescents who have been on medication during their younger years determine that they want to experience who they are without the influence of the medication.

> Many adolescents who have been on medication during their younger years determine that they want to experience who they are without the influence of the medication.

Arthur Robin, an expert on adolescent ADHD, suggests that parents involve their teenagers in decision making.[4] He identifies this participation in decision making as the single most important principle of parenting an adolescent and one of the primary methods of shaping responsible independence behaviors. Adolescents need to be part of the decision-making process about medication. Families who include their teenagers in the decision-making process about medication will find that their teens are more open to discussing the effects of the medication and are more open to continuing if academic or behavioral issues arise. Working closely with families and sharing observations on behavior and academic performance is essential to helping both the family and the individual student make informed decisions about medication and its effectiveness.

While medication can improve impulse control, fine motor control, coordination, restlessness, reaction time, and some short-term memory functions, it is important to realize that medication is not a cure for ADHD.[5] Medication may address some of the core symptoms, but current research finds that it does not address or minimize some of the executive function weaknesses in time management, organization, and effort. Thus, just because a student is taking medication, it does not mean that she will suddenly have an organized binder or no longer need organizational accommodations or additional time for assignments.

Students on medication will need to continue to develop strategies that support them in dealing with some executive function weaknesses.

Responsibilities of the Student

Developing responsibility and self-determination is an ongoing process for teenagers with ADHD. When given the options to classify themselves as smart or not smart, students with ADHD usually put themselves in the "not smart" category. This is due not to any intelligence quotients but to years of academic failures and frustration. These students have not been encouraged to look at academic failures as a learning tool or process. When they make mistakes, they do not try to correct them; they try to hide them. That is often the purpose of the behavior that is seen in the classroom. The student would prefer to be perceived as bad rather than dumb.

Making an Effort and Monitoring Progress

Students with ADHD do not see the direct correlation between effort and good grades because often, despite their best efforts, they have not achieved high marks. Academic achievement has become a gamble, and students don't see the need to pour their energy into activities that are highly unlikely to pay off. The result is a student who is often perceived as unmotivated and lazy. The truth for these students is that there is no purpose for trying harder or attempting to do more when their grades or scores do not reflect their effort. They do not see how grades are related to the real purpose of learning, and they exist in a disconnect due to a faulty feedback system.

Students need direct instruction on how to evaluate their academic progress in order for them to see the correlation between effort and progress. Initially, the teacher needs to budget time to teach this self-reflection process so that students can conduct an error analysis of their own work (see Figure 8.2). This process helps students to see areas of strength and weakness, and they are able to identify in writing the factors that contributed to their performance at the current level. This process takes goal setting to the next level. Here, students determine why goals may not have been met so that they can determine what purposeful activities will help them reach the goal the next time. This process allows students to see a more direct correlation between their actions and their academic outcomes.[6] Examining errors and charting progress with an aimline that shows the closing of the gap between their current achievement and their goal is an effective strategy that increases motivation and promotes student accountability.

> Students with ADHD do not see the direct correlation between effort and good grades because often, despite their best efforts, they have not achieved high marks.

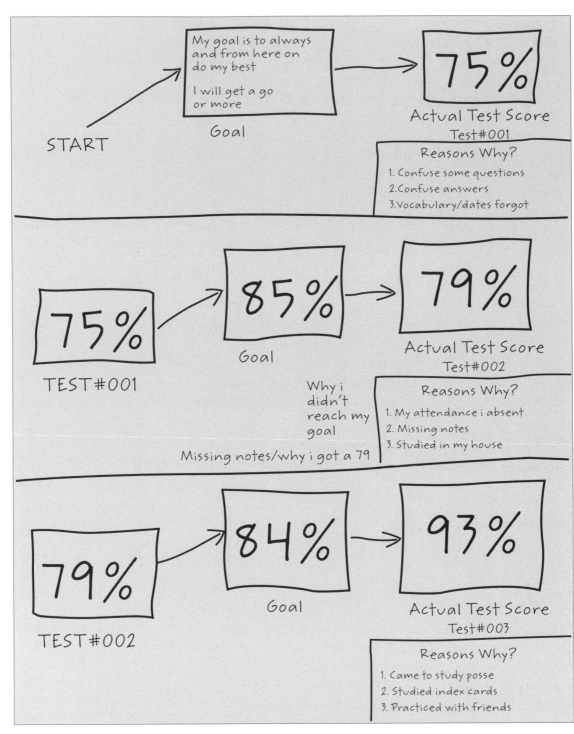

Figure 8.2: Student Self-Reflection on Progress Toward Goal

Source: Copyright © Christopher Lagares. Adapted and used wuth permission.

Once students begin to analyze their errors, they will realize that there are things that they can do that will lessen the feeling that grades are random and arbitrary. Working with a study group rather than studying alone has proven beneficial to many students who have struggled with sustained attention while trying to study. The auditory input and discussion created by a study group supports the cognitive needs of students with ADHD.

When students can narrowly define what effort they have changed or adjusted, they can begin to see that their effort can produce positive outcomes. It is extremely beneficial to helping students realize that they can change outcomes despite their ADHD, that if they use their mistakes to make changes in how they learn, they can move out of the cycle of failure and frustration.

When the connection between making an effort and achieving goals becomes more obvious, students with ADHD take greater responsibility for their own learning. Goal setting becomes more than a futile practice when a student is provided with frequent feedback and an opportunity to analyze errors and adjust goals accordingly. Feedback from report cards and progress reports is not enough to sustain the effort of a student with ADHD.

Using Feedback Constructively

In a meta-analysis of feedback research done by John Hattie and Helen Timperley in 2007 for the Center on Instruction, the findings on the power of feedback were significant, making feedback one of the top five effective instructional methods.[7] They identified types of feedback that helped to close the gap between a student's current level of achievement and the desired level or goal. The helpful types of feedback addressed the following questions:

- Where am I going? (goals)
- How am I going? (progress toward goals)
- Where should I go next? (what must be done to enhance progress toward goals)

In responding to the three questions, feedback may be directed at one of four levels:

- The task
- The processing of the task
- Self-regulation
- The student as an individual[8]

A student with ADHD faced with a specific task would receive feedback on his perceived goal, on his progress on the task, and what he can do to best progress toward the completion of the task. This same type of feedback can be directed at the process he develops to complete the task, on his self-regulation strategies, and on the student as an individual. At the task level, where feedback is most effective, the student is provided with information that lets him know whether he is correct or incorrect or if his interpretation is right or wrong. When student-centered learning occurs, a student can take this information and see the incorrect response as an opportunity to learn; this feedback allows the student to focus on that one area and the strategies that he can use to come to the correct conclusion.

Feedback on the processing level is where many of the strategies in this book are focused. Feedback at the processing level is about having students use strategies to check their work, check through the processes of their work, recognize their own errors, and self-correct. This type of feedback helps students learn to effectively and efficiently use strategies and cues.

As students learn how to use processing-level feedback independently, they begin to develop self-regulation. Feedback on self-regulation helps students to internalize the practice of monitoring their own learning and work, providing internal feedback rather than feedback from others.[9] In this case, the student recognizes an error and goes back through the strategy steps to identify the error and make her own corrections. When the student realizes that through the use of effective strategies, she can take the gamble out of doing well on assignments, she will be more motivated to use these self-regulation strategies and gain greater ownership of her learning. Self-regulation feedback is the most effective feedback because it helps students make the connection between effort and success.

Feedback on the individual level is the least effective type of feedback. This type of feedback is the more global, nebulous "good girl," "great job" kind of statement. This type of feedback does not improve a student's investment of effort or attitude toward learning enough to make a long-term impact. The initial response may be positive, but since the feedback is not specific, it fails to affect achievement. In particular, praising students has been shown to have little or no effect.

The frequency of feedback depends somewhat on the type of feedback provided. Task-level feedback, which is not always immediate, is most effective when provided as quickly as possible. For task feedback to be effective for students with ADHD, especially those with "extra time" accommodations, feedback should be provided at least weekly, if not more often, to allow the student to monitor progress toward the goal and to determine the "what next?" if there is work that needs to be corrected or completed. Process feedback should be immediate, and that is why checking for understanding during classroom instruction is so crucial. When the teacher is able to recognize that a student is headed in the wrong direction, he can direct the student to use a strategy or cue to help herself identify the error and correct it. Positive feedback when students use self-regulation strategies is highly motivating and enhances students' task persistence as well as improves their sense of self-efficacy.[10] Conversely, negative feedback appears to harm the motivation and esteem of students with low self-efficacy. Because many students with ADHD are in the at-risk school population, they often receive more negative feedback than their peers because they often are not efficient at task completion or self-regulation or do not have effective strategies that support them in reaching their goals. Teachers of students with ADHD will need to provide adequate supports to buffer the negative effects that this kind of feedback can have on student motivation.

It is important to point out that feedback is not praise. Praise is often intricately connected with how students view their intelligence.[11] Some students believe that their intellectual ability is a fixed trait, so they might feel that they do not have the intellectual ability to be a successful student. Students with ADHD do not feel very smart, and because nonspecific praise can be an evaluation of a student's intellectual attributes, it may not be an effective tool in bringing about change. Specific praise can be an effective tool when the feedback statement is included in the praise. For example, "You successfully completed five of the seven problems on your homework. I know you worked hard on those. You put forth a good effort." This kind of specific praise and feedback provides data about how the concrete task was accomplished. The student's attributes of being smart are not a part of this equation. Feedback is a tool that provides a reflection of what a student can do, so she can monitor and improve her effort as needed. Perceived attributes and improving them are completely out of the student's control. Therefore, praise based on these attributes is not effective.

In contrast, feedback is about advancing a student's ability to use strategies to monitor their work, self-correct, know when and how to use strategies, and determine when to ask for help.[12] This type of feedback is essential in order for the student with ADHD to be successful in postsecondary endeavors. These strategies can and should be used across all content areas, and when they are used with the other effective strategies discussed in this book, they are more likely to result in improved outcomes for your students with ADHD.

Building Self-Determination Skills

An at-risk student with ADHD often has poor efficacy skills. She does not have strong skills in choice making, decision making, problem solving, goal setting, self-awareness, self-advocacy, or self-regulation. She second-guesses herself and often feels herself a victim of outside forces that she has no control over. The lack of these skills will impede her progress in postsecondary education and in her success as an adult. Developing self-determination skills is essential for this student. Strong academic skills *and* high levels of self-determination are among the variables correlated with positive post-school outcomes.[13] Moira Konrad and her colleagues define self-determination as the "combination of skills, knowledge, and beliefs that enable a person to engage in goal-directed, self-regulated autonomous behavior." Each of these areas is an area of significant concern for a student with ADHD. Direct instruction in goal setting and self-management as well as self-advocacy is necessary for the secondary school student with ADHD to have improved post-school outcomes.

As teachers of students with ADHD, it is crucial that we provide classroom instruction that goes beyond grades and standards met. Students with ADHD and other at-risk populations need interventions that can occur during daily instruction and that will support the development of self-determination skills, given that self-determination and academic achievement go hand in hand. Specifically, instruction in fundamental self-determination skills actually promotes academic skill development.[14] The following strategies are cited by Konrad and her colleagues as ways to promote self-determination skills:

- **Choice making:** Allow students to make choices between academic assignments or the order in which they do assignments (for example, provide a menu of options that allow students who prefer different learning styles to use their strength areas).

- **Decision making:** Teach students to analyze errors and make decisions about actions needed to improve behaviors that support academic performance (for example, study with a partner, use study cards).

- **Problem solving:** Teach skills that support academic achievement and augment academic performance (for example, problem-solving methods, use of mnemonic devices, goal setting with problem-solving steps, evaluating progress on goals, or error analysis).

- **Goal setting:** Teach students to develop goals for the amount and the quality of work they will do (for example, number of problems completed, number of pages read).
  - Use error analysis to develop students' self-regulation strategies, focusing on realistic goal setting.

- **Self-awareness:** Teach students to identify their own strengths and needs pertaining to organization, and develop plans to improve long-term assignment completion by breaking projects into doable parts, monitoring progress, and evaluating quality.
  - Develop students' organizational skills (for example, practice using binders, color-coded plastic accordion folders, and color-coded sticky notes as reminders or putting reminders in cell phone or calendar).
  - Teach students to regularly assess the effectiveness of an organizational strategy to determine whether it works or not.

- **Self-recruiting or self-advocacy:** Teach students to recognize when they need to ask for help.

- Employ the support of the school counselor or other specialist to ensure that each student has a clear understanding of his ADHD and what his accommodations and instructional needs are.
- Teach the student transition skills and educate him on the transition process for his postsecondary school. Understanding the transition process for secondary school is essential to self-advocacy in accomplishing it.

- **Self-regulation and self-management:** Teach students to monitor and reinforce their progress with self-regulated feedback.
  - Teach students to use checklists to monitor their own writing, math problem solving, and problem-solving processes in other subjects.
  - Teach students to record their own progress through check marks or graphing of the completion of parts of assignments.
  - Teach students to evaluate their responses using rubrics.
  - Teach students to use self-talk to instruct themselves through the steps of a task.
  - Teach students to regularly monitor their own progress on goals.
  - Teach students to identify the task for completion, recruit assistance and resources as needed, plan steps to complete the task, and check for accuracy and progress.

Although this list may seem daunting, when students have learned these skills and have a repertoire of strategies under their belt to help them succeed academically, they will be able to have satisfying postsecondary and post-school experiences. They will have the tools needed to make the transition to higher education.

Taking Responsibility for the Postsecondary Transition

As young adults with ADHD make the transition to postsecondary education, it is essential that they have a clear understanding of their disability and their particular needs. The self-determination skills already discussed should help a young adult to have a clear understanding of herself, her needs, and her strengths and to know how to make decisions and set goals. She will need to have developed a clear understanding of how her ADHD affects her academically and behaviorally, as well as a clear picture of her learning style, her academic strengths, and the instructional strategies that work for her.[15] As a student with a disability, it is essential that she know her rights and responsibilities prior to beginning her postsecondary journey.

Many high school students with ADHD have had the support of their parents, counselors, caring teachers, and perhaps other support staff to help them make it through high school. This team approach will not be around when they get to college. A student will need to self-disclose her disability to the designated office on campus so that she can receive the accommodations that she will need in order to be academically successful. College students no longer qualify for special education supports, but they do continue to qualify under Section 504 of the Rehabilitation Act of 1973 as discussed in Chapter One. This act allows students with ADHD equal access to the educational programs of the campus. Section 504 does allow for academic adjustments like extra time to demonstrate mastery, extended time on exams, special seating, and, possibly, a note taker or reader.

Although requirements may vary from campus to campus, in order for a student to obtain the accommodations, she must initiate the process by presenting documentation of her disability and requesting services. Unless she has developed self-advocacy skills, this can be a difficult task. A longitudinal research study conducted by the Office of Special Education Programs of the U.S. Department of Education revealed that two thirds of the students with disabilities interviewed were not receiving accommodations due to a lack of self-disclosure. Half of them did not consider themselves to have a disability, and 7 percent classified themselves as having a disability but chose not to disclose it to the institution that they were attending.[16]

In an article titled "Bridging the Transition Gap From High School to College: Preparing Students with Disabilities for a Successful Postsecondary Experience,"[17] Lynn Gil identifies the student's responsibilities in regard to this important transition:

- Student self-identifies and provides documentation of disability at their own cost.

- The postsecondary institution provides accommodations that do not alter the essential program or course requirements.

- Upon the student's request, disability service providers prepare letters notifying professors of approved accommodations.

- Student must be his or her own advocate for academic needs.

- Postsecondary institutions are not responsible for providing any services that are not available to all students, including personal services or devices.

Why spend this time talking about transition for your students with ADHD? You have worked hard to support them in your classroom by providing them with engaging, differentiated instruction. You have worked with them on their organizational skills. You have provided a safe, positive learning environment; have helped them become self-determined; and have taught them skills and strategies that will support them in higher learning. You do not want all of that effort

Strategies for Teaching Adolescents with ADHD

lost because your student is unwilling to self-disclose or does not understand the transition process.

It is vital that teachers, counselors, and administrators understand that any transition is difficult for any student, but for students with ADHD who struggle with procrastination, getting started, and sustaining effort, this transition can be overwhelming and terrifying. It is the role of the secondary school to ensure that they understand the transition process and know the process steps they will need to take in order to have their needs met.

To Sum Up

This book began with the premise of ADHD expert Chris Zeigler Dendy that it is up to the teacher to make academic success a reality for adolescents with ADHD. You have now read this book, learned about ADHD, improved your pedagogy, created a safe and positive classroom environment, and equipped your students with self-determination and the skills necessary for postsecondary success. It is my hope that this book has provided you with the tools needed to tackle this challenging endeavor. While success for your students with ADHD will not be accomplished without hard work, it is fully worth the effort. Thank you for taking the challenge.

Endnotes

Chapter One

1. Zeigler Dendy, Teaching Teens with ADD and ADHD, 2000.
2. Kongshem, "Failure Is Not an Option," n.d.
3. President's Commission on Excellence in Special Education, A New Era, 2002.
4. Smith, Introduction to Special Education, 2007.
5. Spellings, "Ask the White House," 2006.
6. Cortiella, Rewards and Roadblocks, 2007, p. 6.
7. Algozzine, Ysseldyke, & Elliot, Strategies and Tactics for Effective Instruction, 1997.
8. American Academy of Pediatrics, "ADHD," 2006.

Chapter Two

1. Zeigler Dendy, Teaching Teens with ADD and ADHD, 2000, p. xviii.
2. Ibid.
3. Lougy & Rosenthal, ADHD, 2002; Lougy, DeRuvo, & Rosenthal, Teaching Young Children with ADHD, 2007.
4. Lougy & Rosenthal, 2002.
5. Lougy, DeRuvo, & Rosenthal, 2007.
6. Zeigler Dendy, 2000.
7. Lougy & Rosenthal, 2002.
8. Lougy, DeRuvo, & Rosenthal, 2007.
9. American Psychiatric Association, Diagnostic and Statistical Manual of Mental Disorders, 2000.
10. Zeigler Dendy, 2000.
11. American Psychiatric Association, 2000.
12. Ibid.
13. Ibid.
14. Lougy, DeRuvo, & Rosenthal, 2007.
15. Lahey & Carlson, "Validity of the Diagnostic Category," 1991.
16. Nadeau, Littman, & Quinn, Understanding Girls with ADHD, 1999.
17. Ibid.

18. Ibid.

19. Zeigler Dendy, 2000.

20. Center for the Advancement of Health, "Older Girls with ADHD," 2001.

21. Ibid.

22. Nadeau, Is Your Daughter a Daydreamer?, 2002.

23. Keltner & Woodman-Taylor, "Messy Purse Girls," 2002.

24. Lougy, Rosenthal, & DeRuvo, The School Counselor's Guide to ADHD, 2009.

25. Zeigler Dendy, 2000.

26. Brown, "Executive Functions," 2008.

27. Ibid.

28. Ibid.

29. Ibid.

30. Ibid.

31. Barkley, ADHD and the Nature of Self-Control, 1997.

32. Brown, 2008.

33. Faraone & Kunwar, "ADHD in Children," 2007.

34. Lougy & Rosenthal, "ADHD and Associated Disorders," 2003.

35. American Academy of Pediatrics, "ADHD: What You Need to Know," 2006.

36. Lougy & Rosenthal, 2003.

37. Anastopoulos & Shelton, Assessing Attention-Deficit Hyperactivity Disorder, 2001.

Chapter Three

1. Rutherford, Instruction for All Students, 2008.

2. Ibid.

3. Marzano, Pickering, & Pollock, Classroom Instruction That Works, 2001.

4. Ibid.

5. Conroy, Sutherland, Snyder, & Marsh, "Classwide Interventions," 2008.

6. Lougy & Rosenthal, ADHD, 2002.

7. Center on Instruction, A Synopsis, 2008.

8. Gardner, Frames of Mind, 1993.

9. Dunn & Dunn, Teaching Students, 1978.

10. LdPride.net, "Learning Styles," n.d.

11. Center for Applied Special Technology, "What Is Universal Design for Learning?" n.d.

12. Rutherford, 2008.

13. Individuals with Disabilities Education Improvement Act of 2004.

14. Hunter, Mastery Teaching, 1982.

15. Archer, Keynote speech, 2004.

Chapter Four

1. Doyle, The Learner-Centered Classroom, 2008.
2. Ratey, A User's Guide to the Brain, 2001.
3. Kamil et al., Improving Adolescent Literacy, 2008.
4. Boardman et al., Effective Instruction for Adolescent Struggling Readers, 2008.
5. Biancarosa & Snow, Reading Next, 2004; Perfetti, Landi, & Oakhill, 2005, "The Acquisition of Reading Comprehension Skill," quoted in Boardman et al., 2008.
6. Boardman et al., 2008.
7. Kamil et al., 2008.
8. Boardman et al., 2008.
9. Graves, The Vocabulary Book, 2006.
10. Beck, McKeown, & Kucan, Bringing Words to Life, 2002.
11. Boardman et al., 2008.
12. Ibid.
13. Ibid.
14. Kamil et al., 2008.
15. Guthrie & Humenick, "Motivating Students to Read," 2004.
16. Kamil et al., 2008.
17. Boardman et al., 2008.
18. Zeigler Dendy, 2000.
19. Boardman et al., 2008.
20. Ibid.
21. Ibid.
22. Harris & Graham, Making the Writing Process Work, 1996.
23. Ibid.
24. Ibid.

Chapter Five

1. Fuchs et al., "Prevention, Identification, and Cognitive Determinants," 2005.
2. Mayes & Calhoun, "Frequency of Reading," 2006.
3. Platt, "ADHD and Math Disabilities," 2006.
4. Fuchs et al., "The Cognitive Correlates of Third-Grade Skills," 2006.
5. Swanson & Beebe-Frankenberger, "The Relationship Between Working Memory and Mathematical Problem Solving," 2004.
6. Rittle-Johnson & Star, "Comparing Solution Methods," 2007.
7. Gersten et al., Mathematics Instruction: A Synthesis, 2008.
8. Ibid.

9. Jayanthi, Gersten, & Baker, Mathematics Instruction: A Guide, 2008.

10. Gersten et al., 2008.

11. Butler, Miller, Crehan, Babbitt, & Pierce, "Fraction Instruction," 2003: Witzel, Mercer, & Miller, "Teaching Algebra," 2003.

12. Palincsar, "The Role of Dialogue," 1986.

13. Gersten et al., 2008.

14. Lougy & Rosenthal, ADHD, 2002.

15. Xin, Jitendra, & Deatline-Buchman, "Effects of Mathematical Word Problem-Solving Instruction," 2005.

16. Jayanthi, Gersten, & Baker, 2008.

17. Ibid.

18. Allinder, Bolling, Oats, & Gagnon, "Effects of Teacher Self-Monitoring," 2000.

19. Montague, "Math Problem Solving," 2004.

20. van Garderen & Montague, "Visual Spatial Representation," 2003.

21. Montague, Solve It!, 2003; Montague, Warger, & Morgan, "Solve It!," 2000.

22. Montague, 2003.

23. The Access Center: Improving Outcomes for Students K–8, Using Mnemonic Instruction to Teach Math, n.d. c.

24. The Access Center: Improving Outcomes for Students K–8, Concrete-Representational-Abstract Instructional Approach, n.d. a.

25. Mancini & Gagnon, "Math Graphic Organizers," 2005.

26. Lovitt, "Strategies for Adapting Science Textbooks," 1994.

27. Baxendrall, "Consistent, Coherent, Creative," 2003.

28. Marzano, Pickering, & Pollock, Classroom Instruction That Works, 2001.

29. The Access Center: Improving Outcomes for Students K–8, Strategies for Accessing Algebraic Concepts, n.d. b.

30. Fountas & Pinnell, Guiding Readers and Writers Grades 3-6, 2001, cited in Baxendrall, 2003.

31. Mayes & Calhoun, 2006.

Chapter Six

1. Banilower, Cohen, Pasley, & Weiss, Effective Science Instruction, 2008.

2. Weiss, Pasley, Smith, Banilower, & Heck, Looking Inside the Classroom, 2003.

3. Banilower, Cohen, Pasley, & Weiss, 2008.

4. Ibid.

5. Ibid.

6. Ibid.

7. Hill, "SCORE," n.d.

8. Connor & Lagares, "Facing High Stakes in High School," 2007.

9. Ibid.

10. Ibid.

11. Beers, When Kids Can't Read, 2003.

12. Connor & Lagares, 2007.

13. Teachers Curriculum Institute, "K–12 Curricular Programs," n.d.

14. Connor & Lagares, 2007.

15. Drake & Nelson, Engagement in Teaching History, 2009.

16. Rutherford, Instruction for All Students, 2008.

17. Vygotsky, Mind and Society, 1978.

18. Lougy, DeRuvo, & Rosenthal, Teaching Young Children with ADHD, 2007.

19. Ausubel, "The Use of Advance Organizers," 1960.

20. Drake & Nelson, 2009.

21. Rutherford, 2008.

22. Lougy, DeRuvo, & Rosenthal, 2007.

23. Connor & Lagares, 2007.

24. Sedita, The Key Three Routine, 2008.

Chapter Seven

1. Morrish, With All Due Respect, 2006.

2. Sugai et al., "Applying Positive Behavior Support," 2000.

3. Ibid.

4. Ibid.

5. Morrish, 2006.

6. Canter, "First, the Rapport," 1996, cited in Charles, Building Classroom Discipline, 2005, p. 39.

7. Walker, Shea, & Bauer, Behavior Management, 2004.

8. Lavoie, Learning Disabilities and Discipline, 1996.

9. Walker, Shea, & Bauer, 2004.

10. Ibid.

11. Lavoie, 1996.

12. Levine, A Mind at a Time, 2002.

13. Tangible Time Management, "Time Timer," n.d.

14. Lougy, Rosenthal, & DeRuvo, The School Counselor's Guide to ADHD, 2009.

15. Lavoie, 1996.

16. Ibid.

17. Ibid.

18. Simonsen, Sugai, & Negron, "Schoolwide Positive Behavior Supports," 2008.

19. Horner, Discipline Prevention Data, 2007.

20. Sugai et al., 2000.

21. Horner, 2007.

22. Fairbanks, Simonsen, & Sugai, "Classwide Secondary and Tertiary Tier Practices," 2008.

23. Crone, Horner, & Hawken, Responding to Problem Behaviors, 2004.

24. Ibid.

25. Fairbanks, Simonsen, & Sugai, 2008.

26. Ibid.

Chapter Eight

1. Brown-Chidsey, "No More 'Waiting to Fail,'" 2007.

2. Ibid.

3. Lougy, Rosenthal, & DeRuvo, The School Counselor's Guide to ADHD, 2009.

4. Robin, ADHD in Adolescents, 1998.

5. Lougy, Rosenthal, & DeRuvo, 2009.

6. Connor & Lagares, "Facing High Stakes in High School," 2007.

7. Hattie & Timperley, "The Power of Feedback," 2007.

8. Ibid.

9. Ibid.

10. Ibid.

11. Dweck, "The Perils and Promises of Praise," 2007.

12. Hattie & Timperley, 2007.

13. Konrad, Walker, Fowler, Test, & Wood, "A Model for Aligning Self-Determination," 2008.

14. Ibid.

15. Gil, "Bridging the Transition Gap," 2007.

16. Newman, "Postsecondary Education Participation," 2005.

17. Gil, 2007.

References

Chapter One

Algozzine, B., Ysseldyke, J., & Elliot, J. (1997). *Strategies and tactics for effective instruction*. Longmont, CO: Sopris West.

American Academy of Pediatrics. (2006, Fall). *ADHD: What you need to know*. Retrieved May 14, 2009, from the American Academy of Pediatrics' *Healthy Children* Web site: www.aap.org/healthychildren/06fall/adhd.pdf

Cortiella, C. (2007). *Rewards and roadblocks: How special education students are faring under No Child Left Behind*. Retrieved from National Center for Learning Disabilities Web site: http://www.LD.org

Kongshem, L. (n.d.). *Failure is not an option: An interview with U.S. Secretary of Education Rod Paige*. Retrieved May 14, 2009, from *Scholastic Administrator* Web site: http://www2.scholastic.com/browse/article.jsp?id=75

President's Commission on Excellence in Special Education. (2002). *A new era: Revitalizing special education for children and their families*. Washington, DC: Author.

Smith, D. D. (2007). *Introduction to special education: Making a difference*. Boston: Allyn & Bacon.

Spellings, M. (2006, April 20). *Ask the White House*. Retrieved May 14, 2009, from http://georgewbush-whitehouse.archives.gov/ask/20060420.html

Zeigler Dendy, C. A. (2000). *Teaching teens with ADD and ADHD: A quick reference guide for teachers and parents*. Bethesda, MA: Woodbine House.

Chapter Two

American Academy of Pediatrics. (2006, Fall). *ADHD: What you need to know*. Retrieved May 14, 2009, from the American Academy of Pediatrics' *Healthy Children* Web site: www.aap.org/healthychildren/06fall/adhd.pdf

American Psychiatric Association (2000). *Diagnostic and statistical manual of mental disorders* (4th ed., text rev.). Washington, DC: Author.

Anastopoulos, A. D., & Shelton, T. L. (2001). *Assessing attention-deficit hyperactivity disorder*. New York: Kluwer Academic/Plenum.

Barkley, R. A. (1997). *ADHD and the nature of self-control*. New York: Guilford Press.

Brown, T. (2008, February). Executive functions: Describing six aspects of a complex syndrome. *Attention, 15*(1), 12–17.

Center for the Advancement of Health. (2001, October 12). Older girls with ADHD have more depression, anxiety, smarts. *Science Daily*. Retrieved March 19, 2008, from http://www .sciencedaily.com

Faraone, S. V., & Kunwar, A. R. (2007). ADHD in children with comorbid conditions: Diagnosis, misdiagnosis, and keeping tabs on both. *Medscape Psychiatry and Mental Health*. Retrieved January 20, 2009, from http://www.medscape.com/viewarticle?555748?src=mp

Keltner, N. L., & Woodman-Taylor, E. (2002, April–June). Messy purse girls: Adult females and ADHD. *Perspectives in Psychiatric Care, 38*(2), 69–72.

Lahey, B., & Carlson, C. (1991). Validity of the diagnostic category of attention deficit disorder without hyperactivity: A review of the literature. *Journal of Learning Disabilities, 24*, 110–114.

Lougy, R., DeRuvo, S., & Rosenthal, D. (2007). *Teaching young children with ADHD: Successful strategies and practical interventions for PreK–3*. Thousand Oaks, CA: Corwin Press.

Lougy, R. A., & Rosenthal, D. K. (2002). *ADHD: A survival guide for parents and teachers*. Duarte, CA: Hope Press.

Lougy, R. A., & Rosenthal, D. K. (2003, September/October). ADHD and associated disorders that can affect classroom performance. *The ADHD Challenge, 17*(5), 4–5, 10–11.

Lougy, R. A., Rosenthal, D., & DeRuvo, S. L. (2009). *The school counselor's guide to ADHD: What to know and what to do to help your students*. Thousand Oaks, CA: Corwin Press.

Nadeau, K. G. (2002). *Is your daughter a daydreamer, tomboy or "chatty Kathy"? She may have undiagnosed attention deficit disorder*. Retrieved November 17, 2008, from http://add.org/content/ women/girls.htm

Nadeau, K. G., Littman, E. B., & Quinn, P. O. (1999). *Understanding girls with ADHD*. Silver Spring, MD: Advantage Books.

Zeigler Dendy, C. A. (2000). *Teaching teens with ADD and ADHD: A quick reference guide for teachers and parents*. Bethesda, MA: Woodbine House.

Chapter Three

Archer, A., (2004, February 22). Keynote speech presented at the CARS+ Convention, Palm Springs, CA.

Center for Applied Special Technology. (n.d.). *What is universal design for learning?* Retrieved November 3, 2008, from http://www.cast.org/research/udl/index.html

Center on Instruction. (2008). *A synopsis of Hattie & Timperley's "Power of Feedback."* Portsmouth, NH: RMC Research Corporation.

Conroy, M. A., Sutherland, K. S., Snyder, A. L., & Marsh, S. (2008). Classwide interventions: Effective instruction makes a difference. *Teaching Exceptional Children, 40*(6).

Dunn, R., & Dunn, K. (1978). *Teaching students through their individual learning styles: A practical approach*. Reston, VA: Reston Publishing.

Gardner, H. (1993). *Frames of mind: The theory of multiple intelligences* (10th ed.). New York: Basic Books.

Hunter, M. (1982). *Mastery teaching*. El Segundo, CA: Theory in Practice Publications.

Individuals with Disabilities Education Improvement Act of 2004. Public Law No. 108-446. 2647 Stat. 128. (2004). Retrieved May 16, 2009, from http://idea.ed.gov/download/statute

LdPride.net. (n.d.). *Learning styles and multiple intelligences.* Retrieved November 1, 2008, from http://www.ldpride.net/learningstyles.MI.htm

Lougy, R. A., & Rosenthal, D. K. (2002). *ADHD: A survival guide for parents and teachers.* Duarte, CA: Hope Press.

Marzano, R., Pickering, D., & Pollock, J. (2001). *Classroom instruction that works: Research-based strategies for increasing student achievement.*, Alexandria, VA: Association for Supervision and Curriculum Development.

Rutherford, P. (2008). *Instruction for all students.* Alexandria, VA: Just ASK Publications & Professional Development.

Chapter Four

Beck, I. L., McKeown, M. G., & Kucan, L. (2002). *Bringing words to life: Robust vocabulary instruction.* New York: Guilford Press.

Biancarosa, G., & Snow, C. E. (2004). *Reading next—A vision for action and research in middle and high school literacy: A report to the Carnegie Corporation of New York.* Washington, DC: Alliance for Excellent Education.

Boardman, A. G., Roberts, G., Vaughn, S., Wexler, J., Murray, C. S., & Kosanovich, M. (2008). *Effective instruction for adolescent struggling readers: A practice brief.* Portsmouth, NH: RMC Research Corporation, Center on Instruction.

Doyle, T. (2008, October). The learner-centered classroom: It's not our grandfather's style of teaching. *NEA Higher Education Advocate, 26*(1), 5–8.

Frayer, D., Frederick, W. C., & Klausmeier, H. J. (1969). *A schema for testing the level of cognitive mastery.* Madison: Wisconsin Center for Education Research.

Graves, M. F. (2006). *The vocabulary book: Learning and instruction.* Urbana, IL: Teachers College Press.

Guthrie, J. T., & Humenick, N. M. (2004). Motivating students to read: Evidence for classroom practices that increase reading motivation and achievement. In P. McCardle & V. Chhabra (Eds.), *The voice of evidence in reading research* (pp. 329–354). Baltimore: Brookes.

Harris, K. R., & Graham, S. (1996). *Making the writing process work: Strategies for composition and self-regulation.* Cambridge, MA: Brookline.

Kamil, M. L., Borman, G. D., Dole, J., Kral, C. C., Salinger, T., & Torgesen, J. (2008). *Improving adolescent literacy: Effective classroom and intervention practices: A practice guide* (NCEE No. 2008-4027). Washington, DC: U.S. Department of Education, Institute of Educational Sciences, National Center for Education Evaluation and Regional Assistance.

Kinsella, K. (2003, February 20). *Systematic vocabulary instruction.* Keynote speech presented at the CARS+ Convention, San Jose, CA.

Perfetti, C. A., Landi, N., & Oakhill, H. (2005). The acquisition of reading comprehension skill. In M. J. Snowling & C. Hulme (Eds.), *The science of reading: A handbook* (pp. 227–247). Oxford, UK: Blackwell.

Ratey, J. (2001). *A user's guide to the brain.* New York: Pantheon Books.

Zeigler Dendy, C. A. (2000). *Teaching teens with ADD and ADHD: A quick reference guide for teachers and parents.* Bethesda, MA: Woodbine House.

Chapter Five

The Access Center: Improving Outcomes for Students K–8. (n.d. *a*). *Concrete-representational-abstract instructional approach*. Retrieved November 7, 2008, from http://www.k8accesscenter .org/training_resources/CRA_Instructional_Approach.asp

The Access Center: Improving Outcomes for Students K–8. (n.d. *b*). *Strategies for accessing algebraic concepts (K–8)*. Retrieved November 6, 2008, from http://www.k8accesscenter.org/training _resources/AlgebraicConceptsK-8.asp

The Access Center: Improving Outcomes for Students K–8. (n.d. *c*). *Using mnemonic instruction to teach math*. Retrieved November 7, 2008, from http://www.k8accesscenter.org/training _resources/mnemonics_math.asp

Allinder, R. M., Bolling, R., Oats, R., & Gagnon, W. A. (2000). Effects of teacher self-monitoring on implementation of curriculum-based measurement and mathematics computation achievement of students with disabilities. *Remedial and Special Education, 21*(4), 219–226.

Baxendall, B. W. (2003). Consistent, coherent, creative: The 3 C's of graphic organizers. *Teaching Exceptional Children, 35*(3), 46–53.

Butler, F. M., Miller, S. P., Crehan, K., Babbitt, B., & Pierce, T. (2003). Fraction instruction for students with mathematical disabilities: Comparing two teaching sequences. *Learning Disabilities Research and Practice, 18*, 99–111.

Fountas, I. C., & Pinnell, G. S. (2001). *Guiding readers and writers grades 3–6: Teaching comprehension, genre and content literacy*. Portsmouth, NH: Heinemann.

Fuchs, L., Compton, D., Fuchs, D., Paulsen, K., Bryant, J. D., & Hamlett, C. L. (2005). The prevention, identification, and cognitive determinants of math difficulty. *Journal of Educational Psychology, 97*(3), 493–513.

Fuchs, L., Fuchs, D., Compton, D., Powell, S., Seethlaer, P., Capizzi, A., & Schatschneider, C. (2006). The cognitive correlates of third-grade skills in arithmetic, algorithmic computation and arithmetic word problems. *Journal of Educational Psychology, 98*(1), 29–43.

Gersten, R., Chard, D., Jayanthi, M., Baker, S., Morphy, P., & Flojo, J. (2008). *Mathematics instruction for students with learning disabilities or difficulties learning mathematics: A synthesis of the intervention research*. Portsmouth, NH: RMC Research Corporation, Center on Instruction.

Jayanthi, M., Gersten, R., & Baker, S. (2008). *Mathematics instruction for students with learning disabilities or difficulties learning mathematics: A guide for teachers*. Portsmouth, NH: RMC Research Corporation, Center on Instruction.

Lougy, R. A., & Rosenthal, D. K. (2002). *ADHD: A survival guide for parents and teachers*. Duarte, CA: Hope Press.

Lovitt, S. V. (1994). Strategies for adapting science textbooks for youth with learning disabilities. *Remedial and Special Education, 15*(2), 105–116.

Mancini, P., & Gagnon, J. (2005). *Math graphic organizers for students with disabilities*. Retrieved November 7, 2008, from http://www.k8accesscenter.org/training_resources/ mathgraphicorganizers.asp

Marzano, R., Pickering, D., & Pollock, J. (2001). *Classroom instruction that works: Research-based strategies for increasing student achievement*. Alexandria, VA: Association for Supervision and Curriculum Development.

Mayes, S. D., & Calhoun, S. L. (2006). Frequency of reading, math and writing difficulties in children with clinical disorders. *Learning and Individual Differences, 16*, 145–157.

Montague, M. (2003). *Solve it! A practical approach to teaching mathematical problem solving skills*. Reston, VA: Exceptional Innovations.

Montague, M. (2004). *Math problem solving for middle school students with disabilities*. Retrieved December 15, 2008, from http://www.k8accesscenter.org/training_resources/ MathProblemSolving.asp

Montague, M., Warger, C. L., & Morgan, H. (2000). Solve it! Strategy instruction to improve mathematical problem solving. *Learning Disabilities Research and Practice, 15*, 110–116.

Palincsar, A. S. (1986). The role of dialogue in scaffolded instruction. *Educational Psychology, 21*, 73–98.

Platt, A. (2006). *ADHD and math disabilities: Cognitive similarities and instructional interventions*. Retrieved November 7, 2008, from http://research.aboutkidshealth.ca/teachadhd/ resources/ADHD_and_Math_Disabilities.pdf

Rittle-Johnson, B., & Star, J. R. (2007). Does comparing solution methods facilitate conceptual and procedural knowledge? An experimental study on learning to solve equations. *Journal of Educational Psychology, 99*(3), 561–574.

Swanson, H. L., & Beebe-Frankenberger, M. (2004). The relationship between working memory and mathematical problem solving in children at risk and not at risk for serious math difficulties. *Journal of Educational Psychology, 6*(3), 471–491.

van Garderen, D., & Montague, M. (2003). Visual spatial representation and mathematical problem solving. *Learning Disabilities Research and Practice, 18*, 246–254.

Witzel, B. S., Mercer, C. D., & Miller, M. D. (2003). Teaching algebra to students with learning difficulties: An investigation of an explicit instruction model. *Learning Disabilities Research and Practice, 18*, 121–131.

Xin, Y. P., Jitendra, A. K., & Deatline-Buchman, A. (2005). Effects of mathematical word problem-solving instruction on middle school students with learning problems. *Journal of Special Education, 39*(4), 181–192.

Chapter Six

Ausubel, D. P. (1960). The use of advance organizers in the learning and retention of meaningful verbal material. *Journal of Educational Psychology, 51*, 267–272.

Banilower, E., Cohen, K., Pasley, J., & Weiss, I. (2008). *Effective science instruction: What does the research tell us?* Portsmouth, NH: RMC Research Corporation, Center on Instruction.

Beers, K. (2003). *When kids can't read: What teachers can do. A guide for teachers 6–12*. Plymouth, NH: Heinemann.

Connor, D. J., & Lagares, C. (2007). Facing high stakes in high school: 25 successful strategies from an inclusive social studies classroom. *Teaching Exceptional Children, 40*(2), 18–27.

Drake, F. D., & Nelson, L. R. (2009). *Engagement in teaching history: Theory and practice for middle and secondary teachers*. Upper Saddle River, NJ: Pearson.

Hill, P. (n.d.). *SCORE history/social science: Information literacy*. Retrieved January 2, 2009, from http://score.rims.k12.ca.us/infolit/

Lougy, R., DeRuvo, S., & Rosenthal, D. (2007). *Teaching young children with ADHD: Successful strategies and practical interventions for preK–3*. Thousand Oaks, CA: Corwin.

Rutherford, P. (2008). *Instruction for all students*. Alexandria, VA: Just ASK Publications & Professional Development.

Sedita, J. (2008). *The key three routine: Comprehension strategies™*. Webinar presented at Schools Moving Up, April 9, 2008. Retrieved December 15, 2008, from http://www .schoolsmovingup.net/cs/smu/view/e/2690

Teachers Curriculum Institute. (n.d.). *K–12 curricular programs: History Alive (middle school and high school)*. Retrieved January 2, 2009, from http://www.teachtci.com/programs/

Vygotsky, L. (1978). *Mind and society: The development of higher mental processes*. Cambridge, MA: Harvard University Press.

Weiss, I. R., Pasley, J. D., Smith, P. S, Banilower, E. R., & Heck, D. J. (2003). *Looking inside the classroom: A study of K–12 mathematics and science education in the United States*. Chapel Hill, NC: Horizon Research, Inc.

Chapter Seven

Canter, L. (1996). First, the rapport—then, the rules. *Learning, 24*(5), 12–14.

Charles, C. M. (2005). *Building classroom discipline*. Columbus, OH: Allyn & Bacon, Pearson Press.

Crone, D. A., Horner, R. H., & Hawken, L. S. (2004). *Responding to problem behaviors in school: The behavior education program*. New York: Guilford Press.

Fairbanks, S., Simonsen, B., & Sugai, G. (2008). Classwide secondary and tertiary tier practices and systems. *Teaching Exceptional Children, 40*(6), 44–52.

Horner, R. H. (2007). *Discipline prevention data*. Eugene: University of Oregon, OSEP Center on Positive Behavioral Interventions and Supports.

Lavoie, R. (1996). *Learning disabilities and discipline with Richard Lavoie: When the chips are down . . . Strategies for improving children's behavior, A program guide*. Washington, DC: Learning Disabilities Project at WETA.

Levine, M. (2002). *A mind at a time*. New York: Simon & Schuster.

Lougy, R. A., Rosenthal, D., & DeRuvo, S. L. (2009). *The school counselor's guide to ADHD: What to know and what to do to help your students*. Thousand Oaks, CA: Corwin Press.

Morrish, R. G. (2006). *With all due respect: Keys for building effective school discipline*. Fonthill, Ontario, Canada: Woodstream Publishing.

Simonsen, B., Sugai, G., & Negron, M. (2008). Schoolwide positive behavior supports: Primary systems and practices. *Teaching Exceptional Children, 40*(6), 32–40.

Sugai, G., Horner, R. H., Dunlap, G., Hieneman, M., Lewis T. J., Nelson, C. M., Scott, T., Liaupsin, C., Sailor, W., Turnbull, A. P., Turnbull, H. R., III, Wickham, D., Reuf, M., & Wilcox, B. (2000). Applying positive behavior support and functional assessment in schools. *Journal of Positive Behavioral Interventions, 2*, 131–143.

Tangible Time Management. (n.d.). *Time timer*. Retrieved February 19, 2009, from http://www .timetimer.com/index.php

Walker, J. E., Shea, T. M., & Bauer, A. M. (2004). *Behavior management: A practical approach for educators*. Upper Saddle River, NJ: Pearson Education.

Chapter Eight

Brown-Chidsey, R. (2007). No more "waiting to fail." *Educational Leadership, 65*(2), 40–46.

Connor, D., & Lagares, C. (2007). Facing high stakes in high school: 25 successful strategies from an inclusive social science classroom. *Teaching Exceptional Children, 40*(2), 18–27.

Dweck, C. S. (2007). The perils and promises of praise. *Educational Leadership, 65*(2), 34–39.

Gil, L. A. (2007). Bridging the transition gap from high school to college: Preparing students with disabilities for a successful postsecondary experience. *Teaching Exceptional Children, 40*(3), 12–15.

Hattie, J., & Timperley, H. (2007). The power of feedback. *Review of Education Research, 77,* 81–112.

Konrad, M., Walker, A., Fowler, C., Test, D., & Wood, W. (2008). A model for aligning self-determination and general curriculum standards. *Teaching Exceptional Children, 40*(3), 53–64.

Lougy, R. A., Rosenthal, D., & DeRuvo, S. L. (2009). *The school counselor's guide to ADHD: What to know and what to do to help your students.* Thousand Oaks, CA: Corwin Press.

Newman, L. (2005). Postsecondary education participation of youth with disabilities. In M. Wagner, L. Newman, R. Cameto, N. Garza, & P. Levine, *After high school: A first look at the post-school experiences of youth with disabilities.* A report from the National Longitudinal Transition Study-2. Menlo Park, CA: SRI International.

Robin, A. L. (1998). *ADHD in adolescents: Diagnosis and treatment.* New York: Guilford Press.

Index

Inattention: ADHD indicators regarding, 20; in definition of ADHD, 14–15; of girls with ADHD, 16, 18; during independent practice, 45–46; math difficulties and, 65; signs of, 19; as symptom of ADHD, 15; teacher's directions and, 113

Independent practice: definition of, 45; *versus* group work, 49; lack of student questions during, 115–116

Individualized Education Plan (IEP): accommodations in, 6; in instructional planning, 39–40; legislation affecting, 40

Individuals with Disabilities Education Act (IDEA; 2004), 3, 6

Information literacy, 88–89

Information retrieval, 23

Inhibition, 12, 23–24

Institute of Education Sciences, 50, 51

Instruction for All Students (Rutherford), 28, 93

Instructional scaffolding. *See* Scaffolds

Instructional strategies: considering student behavior in, 108; implementation guidelines for, 38–42; importance of, 27; to increase student engagement, 29–35; lesson design assessment in, 93; linking standards to, 28–29, 39–42; for math, 61–72; to meet academic challenges, 35–37; for science, 86–88, 93–104; for social studies, 88–104. *See also specific strategies*

Integrated instructional approaches, 3, 4

Intelligence, of girls with ADHD, 17

Intensive intervention: description of, 60–61; in English language arts, 60–62; in Response to Intervention process, 123–124

Internal language, 69

Intrinsic motivators, 87

J

Jigsaw strategy, 101–102

K

Key words, 45, 70, 75

Kinesthetic learners. *See* Tactile learners

Kinsella, K., 53, 54

Knowledge: activating prior, 56, 86, 88; assessing prior, 94–95; in math, 66, 76; stored forms of, 33

Kucan, L., 52, 53

K-W-L charts, 88, 95

L

Lab activities, 86–87

Lagares, C., 89–91, 91

Laziness, 14, 116

Learner-centered classrooms: benefits of, 8, 85; collaboration in, 48–49; description of, 7–8; emergence of, 47–48; motivation in, 59–60; ownership of learning in, 49; reading comprehension activities in, 58–59

Learning disabilities, students with: definition of, 5; in math, 65, 82–83; postsecondary education of, 133–135; prevalence of, 25; quality of education provided to, 2; reading interventions for, 60–62; requests for help from, 115–116; school reform legislation and, 2–6; types of, 25

Learning styles: description of, 35–36; in differentiated instruction, 37; inventories for, 36; of teachers, 35

Lecturing: appropriate use of, 98; and emergence of learner-centered classrooms, 48; in social studies and science, 98

Lesson activities, 40–42, 93

Life transitions, 125, 133–135

Linguistic knowledge, 33

Listening, 20

Literacy skills: areas of, 51; goal of, 58; importance of, 50–51; intensive interventions for, 60–62; learner-centered classrooms for, 59–60

M

Major life activities, 5

Manipulatives, 81–82

Manners, 111

Marzano, R., 29, 78

Matching activity, 103–104

Math: accommodations in, 6; disabilities in, 65, 82–83; importance of, 8; instructional principles for, 67–70; instructional strategies for, 71–82; students' challenges in, 76–77, 79–80; types of knowledge in, 66; working memory and, 23

McKeown, M., 52, 53

Medication, 125–127

Memory: executive function and, 21, 23; graphic organizers to support, 33; mnemonic instruction for, 75–76; in social studies, 89–90

Metabolic activity, 12

Middle school transition, 125

Mistakes: ADHD indicators and, 20; oppositional defiance disorder and, 25; routines and, 105; self-regulation of, 130; students' analysis of, 127–129

Mnemonics, 75–76, 80–81

Models: instructional planning and, 42; in math instruction, 67, 68, 74, 78; scaffolding and, 44

Monitoring behavior, 110

Montague, M., 73

Mood disorders, 25

Motivation: during reading instruction, 59–60; in science, 86, 87–88

Motor breaks, 111

Multidisciplinary teams, 123–124

Multiple strategies, 70

Multiple-choice questions: to assess science and social studies, 104; to check for understanding, 45

Multiplication, 68

Rubrics, 42
Rutherford, P., 28, 93

S

Scaffolds: benefits of, 43; function of, 43–44; in math, 76, 78, 80; for note taking, 31, 98–100; for reading comprehension, 56; in science, 96–97, 102, 103, 104; in social studies, 96–97, 102, 103, 104; for summarizing, 102–103; for working memory, 33; in writing, 63
Scavenger hunts, 94
School environment. *See* Positive learning environment
School reform, 2
School, responsibilities of, 122–125
Schoolwide rules, 110, 116–117
Science: instructional strategies for, 86–88, 93–104; main instructional elements of, 86–87; research evidence about, 86–87; students' complaints about, 85
Secondary behavior supports, 110
Section 504 of the Rehabilitation Act of 1973, 3–6, 98, 134
Self-advocacy, 132–133
Self-assessment, 127
Self-awareness, 132
Self-determination, 127, 131–133
Self-disclosure, 134
Self-esteem: development of, 131; of girls, with ADHD, 17
Self-monitoring, 24, 57–59, 127
Self-regulation strategies: for behavior management, 114, 115; to develop self-determination, 133; for English language arts, 62; feedback for, 130; for math, 73
Sense making: description of, 87; in social studies, 89–91
Sensory information, 19
Sequence charts, 77, 78
Sequencing skills: for math, 68, 76, 77, 78; working memory and, 23
Shadow classes, 62
Shame, 18
Short-term memory. *See* Working memory
Shy students, 24
Signals, 109, 111, 113
Silliness, 18
Similarities/differences, identifying: description of, 30; in math, 78, 83; in reading comprehension, 56; in social studies, 89
Sleepy students, 22
Slow-working students, 22
Small-group instruction, 61, 124
Social development: executive function and, 24; of girls, with ADHD, 16, 17; mood disorders and, 25

Social studies: instructional strategies for, 88–104; making meaningful connections in, 89–91; research on, 88–89; students' complaints about, 85
Social withdrawal, 25
Special education: instructional planning for, 40; legislative action affecting, 2–6, 40, 122; Response to Intervention process and, 124
Spellings, M., 2
Standards: in instructional planning, 28–29, 38–42; for writing, 29
Stanford University, 17
Sticky notes, 45
Story maps, 56
Struggling readers: comprehension monitoring of, 57; intensive interventions for, 60–62; motivation of, 59–60; reading discussions of, 59; research on, 50–51
Subtraction, 68
Suffixes, 61
Summarizing: description of, 31; for reading comprehension, 56–57; in science and social studies, 102–103; taking notes for, 99
Summative assessments, 104
Symbols, 90

T

Tactile learners, 36
Take-a-stand strategy, 94–95
Talkative girls, 18
Teachers: acceptance of learner-centered classrooms by, 47–48; accommodation information for, 6; behavior management role of, 108; challenges of, 6–7; in collaborative RtI teams, 124; influence of, 1, 11; learning styles of, 35; recognition of disability by, 7, 14; role of, in direct instruction, 96; in special education *versus* general instruction, 40
Technology: for homework adaptations, 32; students' use of, 7
10:2 rule, 98
Tertiary interventions, 120
Textbooks: instructional planning considerations regarding, 28–29, 39; *versus* visualization strategy, 71
Think-aloud strategies, 67, 68, 74
Thumbs up/down signal, 44–45
Ticket-to-leave strategy, 103
Time: extra, 32, 45, 61, 123; limiting amounts of, during activities, 113–114; sense of, 20; wasting of, 39
Timers, 113–114
Transition words, 103
Transitions, life, 125, 133–135
TREE strategy, 63
Two-column notes, 98–100, 101

U

Unit tests, 104
Universal Design for Learning (UDL), 36–37
University of Virginia, 17
U.S. Department of Education, 134

V

Variables. *See* Algebraic equations
Venn diagram: description of, 30; in math, 78; for reading comprehension, 56
Verbalizing strategies, 69, 70, 74
Violent behaviors, 107
Visual knowledge, 33
Visual learners, 35–36
Visual media: for lectures, 98; for math representations, 76, 81; in problem solving, 69–70; for science, 98; for social studies, 90, 91, 98; for vocabulary instruction, 55
Visualization strategy, 71–72, 73
Vocabulary instruction: explicit strategies for, 52–55; importance of, 51, 52; intensive intervention in, 61
Vygotsky, L., 96

W

Whiteboards, 44
Willful disobedience, 13
Word consciousness, 52
Word problems. *See* Problem solving
Word walls, 53
Working memory: effects of ADHD on, 23; importance of, 23; math difficulties and, 65; scaffolds for, 33; self-regulation strategies for, 62; teacher's directions and, 113
Writing: challenges for students in, 50–51, 62; instructional planning strategies for, 62–63; self-regulation strategies for, 62; standards considerations in, 29; summaries, 102–103

Z

Zero-tolerance policies, 107
Zone of proximal development, 96

Other Books of Interest

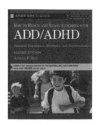

How To Reach and Teach Children with ADD/ ADHD: Practical Techniques, Strategies, and Interventions, 2nd Edition

By: Sandra Rief

ISBN: 978-0-7879-7295-0 | Paperback

The ADHD Book of Lists: A Practical Guide for Helping Children and Teens with Attention Deficit Disorders

By: Sandra Rief | ISBN: 978-0-7879-6591-4 | Paperback

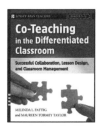

Co-Teaching in the Differentiated Classroom: Successful Collaboration, Lesson Design, and Classroom Management, Grades 5-12

By: Melinda L. Fattig and Maureen Tormey Taylor

ISBN: 978-0-7879-8744-2 | Paperback

ADD/ADHD Behavior-Change Resource Kit:Ready-to-Use Strategies & Activities for Helping Children with Attention Deficit Disorder

By: Grad L. Flick, Ph.D. | ISBN: 978-0-87628-144-4 | Paperback

---

The Six Success Factors for Children with Learning Disabilities: Ready-to-Use Activities to Help Kids with LD Succeed in School and in Life

By: The Frostig Center

ISBN: 978-0-470-38377-3 | Paperback

Differentiated Instruction for the Middle School Language Arts Teacher: Activities and Strategies for an Inclusive Classroom

By: Joan D'Amico and Kate Gallaway | ISBN: 978-0-7879-8466-3 | Paperback

---

Supported Literacy for Adolescents: Transforming Teaching and Content Learning for the 21st Century

By: Catherine Cobb Morocco, Cynthia Mata-Aguilar, Carol J. Bershad

ISBN: 978-0-470-22269-0 | Paperback

Other Books Published in Partnership with WestEd

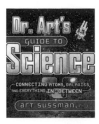

Dr. Art's Guide to Science: Connecting Atoms, Galaxies, and Everything in Between

By: Art Sussman, Ph.D. | ISBN: 978-0-7879-8326-0 | Hardcover

Mentoring Teachers Toward Excellence: Supporting and Developing Highly Qualified Teachers

Judith H. Shulman and Mistilina Sato, Editors

ISBN: 978-0-7879-8434-2 | Hardcover

The Reading Apprenticeship Framework

Reading for Understanding: A Guide to Improving Reading in Middle and High School Classrooms

By: Ruth Schoenbach, Cynthia Greenleaf, Christine Cziko, Lori Hurwitz

ISBN: 978-0-7879-5045-3 | Paperback

Building Academic Literacy: An Anthology for Reading Apprenticeship

Audrey Fielding and Ruth Schoenbach, Editors | ISBN: 978-0-7879-6555-6 | Paperback

---

Building Academic Literacy: Lessons from Reading Apprenticeship Classrooms, Grades 6-12

Audrey Fielding, Ruth Schoenbach, and Marean Jordan, Editors
ISBN: 978-0-7879-6556-3 | Paperback

Rethinking Preparation for Content Area Teaching: The Reading Apprenticeship Approach

By: Jane Braunger, David M. Donahue, Kate Evans, and Tomás Galguera
ISBN: 978-0-7879-7166-3 | Hardcover